PRAISE F
W

"You will find yourself in this book. Each story spoke to me in a different way. In a time when we need community the most, this book made me feel less alone and more hopeful than ever."

–Dana Malstaff, CEO, Boss Mom LLC

"Through Marta Spirk's inspiration and leadership, a tremendous group of women was brought together to share their journeys in *The Empowered Woman's Path*. Their insights and encouragement will allow anyone to have the courage to embark on their own personal journey. A must read!"

–Gary Barnes, International Speaker, Serial Entrepreneur, and Traction Business Coach at GaryBarnersInternational.com

"*The Empowered Woman's Path: Inspiring Stories of Success in Life & Business*, is an incredible journey from dreams to reality. This collaborative book beautifully weaves together the stories of 21 remarkable women who have walked the path toward self-empowerment. This book isn't just for entrepreneurs; it's for anyone seeking inspiration and empowerment in their life journey. The stories highlight the transformative power of resilience, community, and mentorship. These women have disrupted norms, created opportunities, and paved the way for future generations of leaders."

–Natalie Tysdal, Emmy Award Winning Journalist and TV Anchor, Host of the Natalie Tysdal Podcast

"This book is a powerful reminder that where you are today is the first step on your growth journey to becoming the woman of your dreams. Marta is an example of someone who walks her talk! Watching Marta's growth over the years has been nothing short of inspirational. She's evolved through finding her voice, to leading with her voice, to now using her voice to empower others."

–Lisa Simone Richards, PR and Visibility Strategist at LisaSimoneRichards.com

"Marta Spirk's *The Empowered Woman's Path* is a transformative masterpiece that every woman should read. Each chapter is a journey through self-discovery and empowerment that I found incredibly relatable. The section titled "Listen to Yourself" resonated with me deeply. Listening to our inner voices is critical for making decisions that align with our authentic selves, which is invaluable no matter your line of work or life circumstances. And let's talk about "Forgive Yourself" and "Empower Yourself"—these chapters aren't just inspirational, they're foundational. They get to the core of self-belief and resilience, attributes that everyone could use more of in their lives. Trust me, *The Empowered Woman's Path* will not just inspire you—it will change you."

–Rebeca Lima, Business Coach and Strategist at RebecaLima.Coach

The EMPOWERED WOMAN'S Path

21 INSPIRING STORIES OF SUCCESS IN LIFE & BUSINESS

BY

MARTA SPIRK & CO-AUTHORS

Published by Mom Does It All LLC

Copyright 2023 Marta Spirk

Printed in the United States of America

Paperback ISBN: 979-8-9850925-3-0
Hardcover ISBN: 979-8-9850925-5-4

Marta Spirk & Co-Authors, The Empowered Woman's Path

Disclaimer/Warning:

This book is dedicated to every woman who is ready to embrace all that they are, so they can become the empowered woman within.

CONTENTS

INTRODUCTION

*I*F YOU WANT to feel simultaneously terrified and loved beyond words, publish a book. After years of wanting to become an author, I finally realized my dream in January 2022. The amount of support I received was incredible, but the winding road to that moment started a few years before.

Leading up to the troubled year of 2020, I had been facing resistance from my family and my own fears regarding my business. I felt unclear on the direction I should take and didn't have much in the way of results to show since starting back in 2016. In a desperate attempt to find my way—mid-pandemic—I jumped into a coaching course and was asked to develop my own coaching method and framework. I scraped together some ideas and decided to call it The Empowered Woman's Path, a few steps to help women entrepreneurs empower themselves through any situation.

What seemed like a completely made-up personal growth system turned out to be much more. When I finally decided to move forward with writing a book, I knew just how to organize it: I'd use the steps I created a few months back.

When insecurities and impostor syndrome tried to overwhelm me, I finally decided to seek help—I spoke the contents of each chapter into my phone and sent it all to a ghostwriter. Soon, the short, but sweet, manuscript was ready for the editor. In about three months, it was sent for publishing. *The Empowered Woman: The Ultimate Roadmap to Business Success* was born.

Since then, the book has reached best-seller status in Women & Business and several other categories, with thousands of copies sold all over the world. It has also been recognized with an EVVY award in the business category by the Colorado Independent Publishers Association (CIPA).

Two months after the initial release, I also got to step on the prestigious TEDx stage and share the same steps of The Empowered Woman's Path with a large audience.

This is the story of how, in just a couple of years, The Empowered Woman's Path went from a coaching exercise scribbled onto pages to a best-selling book and a talk on TED's website. I could have never imagined it like this, but I did dream it. Even when it seemed there was no room or opportunity for this Brazilian-born, triplet mom to share her voice, I kept on pressing forward. All my connections and network were in Brazil, and my American family didn't always understand my vision for my business, but after having my triplets, I felt a pull to start something new, and it wouldn't leave me alone.

I kept on walking that path toward my self-empowerment.

And on the way, I was able to triple my income, reaching multiple six figures in sales. At the same time, I increased my client base, following, and reach. As I've refined my message, I have mentored my clients to identify and move past visibility blocks, such as impostor syndrome, comparison, and fears, so their brands and businesses can reach greater awareness and exposure. It's been rewarding to watch transformations happening right before my eyes, knowing I have been an active part of it all. Some of these women have started new businesses, launched new programs, hosted in-person events, stepped on large stages, and much more—all because, through each obstacle and achievement I've faced, I never gave up. I've held on to my dream of impacting women and witnessing their positive ripples within their families and communities.

And now, I get to use this collaboration book as a vehicle to show you that I'm not the only one.

The women you're about to meet have walked the path toward self-empowerment, themselves, and have left their marks with their life stories and businesses. They have held the vision of greater impact by sharing *their* voices, which is why their stories must be heard. And now, as *The Empowered Woman's Path: 21 Inspiring Stories of Success in Life & Business* is born, their stories will be heard.

After throwing the idea of a collaboration book out there to my clients and network, I was pleasantly surprised to see how many were interested in writing a chapter with me. This response, in itself, helped me put my own journey into perspective and acknowledge the impact I've created through the years.

Some of these women are long-time clients and friends, while others came via mutual connections. Soon, we had a group of 21 powerhouses from different walks of life, business stages, and industries. All of them bring touching life experiences and breakthroughs into these pages.

Once they began writing their drafts, my next challenge was to create a structure for the book to do justice to each author's uniqueness. And then the obvious answer hit me: I'll use the same steps outlined in my first book!

Throughout these pages, you will find five parts that contain chapters written by different women. Following the framework I created in 2020, we will move through Notice Yourself, Listen to Yourself, Forgive Yourself, Empower Yourself, and finally, Transform Yourself.

In the beginning of each part, I will present a brief description of that particular step, which I explain in-depth in my first book, and will also share a short personal introduction to the authors and their chapters within that section.

Whether you are an aspiring or current entrepreneur, or perhaps a career woman looking to become empowered, get ready to witness the transformative power of resilience outlined by the 21 chapters that follow. These women's stories will inspire you to navigate the uncharted waters of life and entrepreneurship with courage and determination. You will witness the power of community and mentorship, as these women leaned on the support of others to overcome challenges and drive their businesses forward. Most importantly, you will witness the profound impact that women entrepreneurs can have on society, as they disrupt norms, create employment opportunities, and pave the way for future generations of aspiring business leaders.

Be prepared to be moved, motivated, and inspired. Take some time to look over the About the Authors section at the end of the book, where you will find details on each of these women's businesses and contact information.

Reach out to them and let them know how their story has impacted you to carry this empowerment movement through.

My hope is that, together, we make it a habit and priority to celebrate one another's accomplishments, honor each other's unwavering determination, and unlock the untapped potential within ourselves. May these stories ignite a flame within you, urging you to embark on your own empowering journey, walking down The Empowered Woman's Path. And as we lock arms, let us usher in a new era where empowered women thrive and reshape the world by empowering themselves—and each other—along the way.

PART

1

NOTICE YOURSELF

*A*S I DESCRIBED in *The Empowered Woman: The Ultimate Roadmap to Business Success*, Noticing Yourself is the first step toward self-empowerment because it focuses on learning who you truly are—what makes you unique—so that you can embrace it and *be* it. In order to own your individuality and live a life that's authentic to you, it's important to take interest in yourself. The chapters that follow in this part showcase the power of taking the time to *notice yourself*.

Janae Andrus Cox is one of the women I've known the longest in this collaboration book. We met at my very first conference for entrepreneurs in the spring of 2019. She drove into Denver from Idaho for the event, and among hundreds of participants, we ended up in the same group during a networking activity. I was so amazed by her drive, especially leading a product-based business. I'd known the challenges of promoting my coaching services, and I could only imagine the intensity that tackling the manufacturing and marketing of a physical product entailed. We stayed connected through the years, and now her life and business story open this book. She beautifully outlines how many of us struggle to recognize our own gifts and how, with time, by committing to the practice of noticing ourselves, we can take steps toward sharing our wisdom with the world.

Randi Jo Pieper is one of the most giving women I've had the pleasure to meet and work with. She saw me speak at a women's conference put together by the Brighton Chamber of Commerce in Colorado, as she's had a long-time career serving as a probation officer for Adams County, Brighton's home. After getting a copy of my book at the event, she reached out on social media and, soon, joined some of my programs. I am so proud of her for stepping out and speaking at one of my events about her caretaker journey. Now, this incredible woman has her own contribution in this book, shining light on the highs and lows of having a caretaker role.

Up next is **Anna Cheney**. We connected through a mutual friend and client who is also a contributing author in this book, Vesta Hager. In her chapter, she describes the definition of Enneagram 2, the Helper. Whether you identify with this personality type or not, as women, especially as moms and caretakers, we deeply understand the challenge of putting ourselves first. In Anna's case, this challenge culminated with her own daughter calling her out for putting everyone else before her own needs, resulting in self-abandonment. I'm confident you will be moved by her words.

Finally, **Terri Mongait**, a remarkable woman with such a memorable story and mission, joins the book. I met Terri at a networking meeting in the summer of 2022 and had the pleasure of seeing her work in action. I visited her Begin Again Ranch in Sedalia, Colorado, where she partners up with her horses to help people uncover the stories keeping them stuck. Her chapter closes this part by addressing past wounds that can impact the way you see yourself and, therefore, the way you show up in the world.

TOUCH & TELL:
BECOMING A CONNECTION EXPERT

By Janae Andrus Cox, CCM, PMP, MBA

*A*S A CONNECTION expert, though I do have all the formal higher education, degrees, and certifications, I firmly believe my strongest qualifications that made me an expert came through informal education first.

What is a connection expert? A connection expert can be relied upon to see what is missing in an unsuccessful interaction where connection isn't achieved; they understand the ingredients that go into creating deep and lasting connections. This expertise can be applied in both business and personal relationships. I have personally utilized my expertise in my career in many capacities, from doing community work for tech companies to bringing executives together to running open-source communities to help users connect. My work has led me to assist others in learning to run more effective teams and aid couples in reaching a deeply rewarding connection in their relationships.

You may be in a position where you have developed expertise informally and are struggling to recognize yourself as an expert. My message to you is to not limit your definition of expertise to formal education. It was prior to most of my formal education that I used my expertise to develop a card game for couples to increase emotional intimacy and improve conversation and connection in relationships. Touch & Tell is the genesis of that effort and serves as a powerful tool for couples to connect. I have spent a lifetime honing the skills needed to create it. So many entrepreneurs, business owners, and professionals struggle with "imposter syndrome". This can be a very limiting internal struggle. It will never matter how much success you achieve externally if you cannot allow yourself to embrace success internally. While I did, ultimately, go and obtain the official qualifications readily recognized by society, I was a connection expert before earning a graduate degree. Once I recognized that expertise in myself, I was unstoppable.

The foundations for my expertise began to be put in place two days before I was born, when my father joined the United States Air Force. By the time I left home at the age of seventeen, I had moved eleven times. Needless to say, I learned very quickly how to form meaningful relationships quickly and navigate all kinds of different people and cultures.

Building connections was not a casual undertaking for me and my brothers, as we had to navigate new social circles with serious intention if we were going to have any friends at each new place. My older brother and I often had long talks about how to integrate into unfamiliar social circles and shared thoughts on who we could probably count on as friends. I have countless memories of sitting at the end of my brother's bed, listening to him talk through a social scenario at the end of the day. Though making friends in this way was challenging, I always had my brothers during all our moves.

Moving eleven times didn't just give me exposure to different cultures, but also gave me ample exposure to different social experiences. In Germany, I had a large group of close friends and was a natural leader. I was a dedicated student and built great relationships with my teachers. In California, I had a couple of good friends, but was bullied at school. My teachers thought I wasn't a very engaged student because I was quieter in order to avoid the bullies, and so my grades suffered, as well. In Texas, I was very social. I had lots of friends and dated several great guys—and my grades were decent. In Washington, I was considered a nerd. I was a top student and graduated early with college credits but didn't have many friends. I changed very little about myself from place to place, but the way I fit into different environments was unique to each place and created unique experiences for me. These varied experiences have empowered me to relate to people from many backgrounds. Were you popular, bullied, smart, lonely, quiet, loud, successful in school? Did you struggle with academics? Did you live in a small town? Were you a student at a large school or a small school? To all of these questions, I can answer, "Me, too."

Living in several different countries required me to acclimate to cultural nuances quickly. I remember noticing—early and often—that it didn't matter what language someone spoke; we all experienced the same spectrum of human emotions. It became clear to me that I could always connect with someone if I could relate to them emotionally. Connection is a human experience, and we are only limited by our culture or language if we fail to navigate our differences with grace and open communication.

For example, when I was a young girl living on the island of Terceira, I spent time with the family who owned the farmhouse we were renting. We spoke very little Portuguese, and they spoke very little English. I sat with their daughter, Fabiana, and I will never forget the strong connection we were able to build without any words. We smiled and gestured as we exchanged necklaces. She was thrilled with the smiley face choker I gave her, and I was enraptured by the beautiful pink crystal necklace she gave me. We shared our cultures and our interests and friendship without any words. This experience gave me a powerful example of connection and was formative in my understanding of how we can connect with each other in unique ways.

Through all of these situations, I learned to read people. I learned to ask the right questions to understand who people were at their core, beyond the standard small talk that didn't truly get me what I needed. I learned to let go when I needed to and to hold on when I wanted to. I learned to maintain connections even after moving away and to say "see you later" instead of "goodbye". And, most painfully of all, I began to learn that genuine connection is a two-way street.

When I was 20 years old, I married a 26-year-old man who had captured my interest at a political convention two years prior. He was everything I had been told I was supposed to look for: educated, well-employed, church-going, and polite. My parents approved. I had a nagging feeling that his lack of affection toward me was a deeper issue than what he explained away as being introverted, and it was certainly a red flag that he wouldn't allow me to tell even my closest friends that he had been married before. He was closed off, to say the least, but I was sure it was temporary and that I would love him enough to change that.

The stage was set: a young, passionate woman who was convinced she would help her new husband open up and have a beautiful life with her, and a quiet, intentional man who had no inclination to do any such thing.

As a young bride, now married to a man who approached marriage as a division of traditional roles and did not see emotional intimacy as part of the package, I was determined to convince him of the beauty and power of connection. I was so sure if I just turned the right key, I could make the difference. After forming so many unconventional connections in my life, surely if anyone could reach him, it was me. Over the next eight years, I tried everything I could conceive: reading every marriage book I could get my hands on, Googling everything I could think of about relationships, listening to love songs like it was research, trying to be more docile, trying to be more firm, listening to audio books on relationships, attending conferences for wives, seeking religious support, meeting with therapists and counselors individually and as a couple, researching love languages, having a regular date night, trying new things in the bedroom, asking his mother for help, and asking God for help. I tried writing letters to him as memos and using business terminology to connect to his logical side. I even tried not initiating conversation with him and told him that I would let him come to me on his terms when he was ready, but then no one spoke in our house for three days until I was so lonely that I caved and broke the silence.

When I finally admitted to myself that I needed to let go, I knew what to do, but I struggled in feeling that all those efforts had been fruitless. Then a powerful thing happened. The night before our divorce proceedings, I got a phone call from my soon-to-be-ex-husband, who wanted to make sure I knew that he never loved me in the ten years he had known me. It didn't hurt to hear. It was the most honest thing he had ever said to me, and my heart was grateful for the truth. You cannot water a dead plant and expect it to grow, which is what I had—inadvertently—been doing. But, if you're motivated enough to attempt to revive a dead plant, you will become an expert gardener before you realize that nothing will work for this particular plant. Imagine the garden you will grow when you finally water living seeds with all those hard-learned skills! I couldn't see that yet. It would be many months before I would realize the expertise my struggles had honed in me. But, ultimately, I benefited from all that hard work, fruitless as it seemed at the time.

Dating after my first marriage was something I approached with my walls up. I met many wonderful people, but I kept everyone at a distance. I was not looking for a close connection yet. Then, a charismatic Englishman asked me to lunch, and I agreed. He was different. He asked me the most disarming and insightful questions, and I was captivated. After several weeks of regular dates, I wanted to open up and really connect with this guy, and so I leveraged my innate understanding of how to connect genuinely and decided to try something unique. I shopped around for conversation cards to prompt deeper conversations. Unfortunately, everything I looked at fell short of my expectations and didn't match what I knew would foster true connection.

So, I decided to make my own.

I started jotting down conversation-starter ideas, tapping into the vast mental library I'd accumulated from a lifetime of forming connections and nearly a decade of deep digging to nurture a dead relationship. The ideas flowed out of me naturally, with that wealth of knowledge readily available to fuel my drive to find a genuine connection that I could count on.

An interesting thing happened as those wheels turned over all I had learned. One of the questions was a particularly vulnerable one because it asked him to share about a loved one that had passed away. I realized it was a question that could potentially be difficult for him to speak about, and it would work better if I could facilitate that vulnerability with a more receptive environment. I added a note to hold hands during that discussion, and then I started thinking about what other touches I could incorporate to really encourage the flow of oxytocin during the game, leveraging biology and psychology to facilitate bonding between the partners.

I glanced through the existing cards and easily thought of more touches that coordinated with each discussion prompt. I wrote a card that said, "Rub your partner's arms from behind while they tell you what makes them feel strong." Another card, a personal favorite: "Run one finger along the length of your partner's body while giving them a compliment about something non-physical that you admire about them."

I found that I had several layers of understanding of how each of the cards would be able to optimize vulnerability and invite the release of oxytocin to truly create a genuine bond already present in my own experiential knowledge. I jotted down "Touch & Tell" on the first card and brought my game to my date. I had no idea that I had just created something that would improve so many relationships beyond my own.

The game was a hit, and I felt an incredible bond and connection with this man. I remember how he put his arms around me at the end of the date to say goodbye, and I just knew there was something special there. Was it him? Was it the game-fostered connection? Was it both? I wasn't sure yet. His friend asked if he could borrow the game and later told me that it had helped him connect with his wife in a unique and powerful way. I loved hearing that. My other friends started to ask to borrow the game, and I got more rave reviews. I knew then that I had created something special out of my experiences.

The Englishman and I ultimately didn't remain connected on a romantic level, and though we went our separate ways, we remain on good terms. The connection and love I was able to feel with him is something I'll always appreciate him for and was a pivotal experience in me being ready to marry the love of my life years later— but that is another story.

As I continued to work on Touch & Tell, I discovered over and over again how impactful Touch & Tell was for couples. My twenty cards, written with sharpie on index cards, had since evolved into an enormous 250-card deck. The couples who completed the field testing came back with glowing reviews that warmed my heart. Hearing their stories fueled me to push through all the pains of starting my own business and navigating manufacturing, shipping, and fulfillment. I learned so much as I pushed through some of the most difficult portions of those early business days.

I enrolled in a business entrepreneurship course to support my professional development, and I remember other students in the course asking me, incessantly, when my product was going to be on the market so that they could use it at home. They had seen my mockups and used some sample cards, and they were eager for more. Those kinds of reminders showed me that I was doing something much-needed in helping others find the deeper connection that couples crave. I knew so well how hard relationships could be, and while doing the work is important in relationships, I wanted to make the work fun!

Once Touch & Tell hit the market, it didn't take long to go from my best friend ordering the very first copy while we were on the phone together to hearing that my game was circulating among the faculty in several university psychology departments. I know the game is powerful, but it always lights me up inside when I hear a new success story. I've had older mothers thank me for giving them a way to support their adult children in their marriages in a non-intrusive way. I've had therapists tell me that they won't even meet with their clients for couples counseling until they have played the game together because it lays such a valuable foundation for connection. I have had a customer track me down online to personally thank me for the game that saved his marriage.

I became a connection expert through nearly thirty years of life experiences, and seeing that expertise flow out of me in a way that was impactful for others was a powerful experience. Though I had already become an expert in my own right, I was eager to formalize some of my expertise as I continued to learn and grow. Some of my knowledge was shaped by my undergraduate education, but I dreamed of being able to earn an MBA.

Unfortunately, at first, I couldn't afford to go back to school. So, I looked up various curriculums and found the most read books in MBA programs. As a birthday gift to myself, I splurged and bought as many of those business books as I reasonably could. I devoured those books over the next couple of years until I knew them inside and out. At the time, it felt like such an insignificant thing, and I lamented not being able to be enrolled in a formal education program. However, when I did have the means to be able to enroll in an MBA program, I found a self-paced program that recommended two and a half years to complete the degree. I completed it in seven months.

I already knew so much of the material from my reading and my experience. I realized that I had been underestimating my years of building expertise on my own. I thought my MBA would be a deep learning experience, but it turned out to be putting the formal cherry on top of hard-won education I'd already earned independently. It is critical to not underestimate the education you gain through informal channels; I had a similar experience when I earned my certification as a conflict manager (CCM) and found that I had already studied the majority of the material in the course through my own deep study of connection. I will always advocate for formal education, but I will advocate even harder to choose to be a student no matter what university of life you are in.

Recognizing your own expertise and allowing yourself to become a student of life are the key ways that you become a successful expert in your field. None of this can be achieved if you aren't taking the time to check in with yourself to acknowledge how far you have come and what you have already gained expertise in throughout your life. Allow that success to resonate internally so that you can continue to pursue success externally, as well. If you're going to make it as an expert in any field, in my expert opinion, the best person you can connect to is yourself.

UNLEASHING THE CARETAKER'S POTENTIAL: A JOURNEY TO EMPOWERMENT

By Randi Jo Pieper

THIS CHAPTER IS not just about my journey; it is an invitation for all caretakers to embark on their own transformative paths. It is never too early or too late to reclaim our power and embrace our dreams. As Henry Ford once said, "Whether you think you can or you think you can't—you're right."[1] It is time for us to believe in ourselves and step into our greatness.

I guess you could say I have been a caretaker since the age of three or four. It all started when my mom underwent back surgery and my little sister was diagnosed with celiac disease. From that moment on, my life revolved around taking care of my family or believing I needed to. Looking back on why I felt such a strong urge to care for my family,

---

[1] Ford, Henry. "Henry Ford > Quotes." Goodreads. Accessed September 12, 2023. https://www.goodreads.com/author/quotes/203714.Henry_Ford.

I find myself tracing it to my position as the eldest among three sisters and my status as a "miracle child". My parents had endured the heartache of losing two children through stillbirth before my arrival—a backdrop that significantly influenced my perspective.

Growing up, this unique family history, coupled with the challenges my mother faced due to her back surgery and my sister's diagnosis of celiac disease, fostered a deep-seated sense of responsibility within me. The values instilled by my father and grandparents, encouraging me to always be helpful and supportive, have been etched into my memory since as far back as I can recall, even dating back to when I was about three years old. But little did I know, this selfless act of love would eventually leave me feeling stuck, yearning to grow and unleash my full potential.

As the years passed, I found myself shouldering more responsibilities. I witnessed my dad turning to alcohol as a coping mechanism, especially when his parents started aging and my beloved grandmother, Nettie, passed away. These were pivotal moments that shaped my understanding of the world and my role in it.

Being the eldest among my siblings, I naturally assumed the role of mediator during my parents' conflicts. This often placed me in a difficult position, particularly when my father would frequent the bar. I distinctly recall an instance from my childhood, when I was around seven years old. During those times, my father would be at the bars, engrossed in selling farm equipment and pickups to fellow farmers. However, when it was time for supper, I found myself tasked with a peculiar responsibility.

I can still vividly remember picking up the phone, my small hands dialing the bar's number. With a sense of youthful innocence and responsibility, I would inquire about my father's whereabouts and estimate when he might return home to join us for supper. It wasn't uncommon for me to stay up well past my bedtime, eagerly awaiting the sound of the front door creaking open, a telltale sign that my father had returned home safely from the bar.

As the years passed throughout elementary, junior, and high school, much was unchanged. One defining experience occurred during my teenage years when I underwent an assessment at a job service agency. It was meant to guide me toward a suitable career path. At just nineteen years old, hearing the results felt like a slap in the face. The assessment score labeled me as fit only for warehouse work on an assembly line. How could this be? I had dreams, ambitions, and a strong support system consisting of my parents and grandparents, who believed in me.

Determined to prove them wrong, I embarked on a journey of self-discovery. I yearned to find my true calling and break free from the limitations imposed by a single assessment. I explored various paths, from nursing, like my mother, to teaching, like my grandmother and uncle, and even child psychology. Each pursuit was driven by a thirst to taste everything life had to offer.

In search of guidance, I sought assistance from the job service once again, hoping to find better clarity about my strengths and potential career paths. While sitting in an older man's office, I eagerly awaited my assessment scores one more time, hoping to find the key to unlocking my future. But the results shattered my hopes once again.

The man looked at me and said, "Randena, your score indicates that your best career option is *still* working in a warehouse on an assembly line."

I distinctly remember sitting in that drab, beige-walled office as those words hit me like a ton of bricks. The fluorescent lights flickered overhead, casting a sickly pallor on the worn-out carpet that had seen better days, and the faint aroma of stale coffee clung to the air like a persistent ghost.

I tell ya—I mean, seriously—how could they just boil down all that I am into such a narrow box? It was like a punch in the gut, the kind that leaves you winded and wondering what the heck just happened. I've always been the go-getter, the one juggling school, clubs, church stuff, and even my gig as a shift manager at freakin' McDonald's. But there I was, standing like some lost puppy, being told that, apparently, I was only good for one thing.

My heart was pounding harder than a bass drum at a rock concert—ba-dum, ba-dum, ba-dum—syncing up with the ticking of that ancient wall clock. It was like time was mocking me, daring me to figure things out right then and there.

And that piece of paper in my hand was like holding a piece of my future—crinkled and uncertain. The edges were rough, like it had been through its fair share of battles, just as I was about to go through. My fingertips could feel every bump and crevice, and that paper was transferring all its doubt and frustration onto me.

But amidst the clinical atmosphere, the taste of disillusionment, and the muffled drone of office chatter, a spark ignited within me. It was a spark that crackled and danced, defying the sterility of the environment around me. The scent of determination, like a whiff of fresh air after a rain shower, crept into the room, carrying with it a promise that I was more than just a cog in this bureaucratic machine.

I refused to let those soul-crushing words define my worth. I refused to let the limited scope of this office dictate the breadth of my potential. The room might have been suffocating, the taste might have been bitter, but within me, a fire blazed—a fire that would incinerate the confines of mediocrity and illuminate a path to my true purpose.

As time passed, I pursued higher education while juggling work at my folks' restaurant and Walmart, steadily climbing the ladder toward management. After I graduated from college and went on to become a probation officer, my career hit a wall after seven years. I yearned for growth, longing to step into a managerial position, yet despite numerous attempts over a decade, I couldn't break through. Frustration and disappointment seeped into my spirit, leaving me questioning why I seemed destined to remain stagnant and not climb the ladder. Back then, from where I stood, climbing the career ladder was pretty much about the moolah, you know?

Of course, there was also this burning desire to give my family a better shot at life. I had an itch to be that gal who carves her own path and leaves a legacy. And oh boy, let's not forget that old dude at the "Job Service" office. I was hell-bent on showing him that I was way more than just a cog in their bureaucratic machine, destined to slave away on a dull assembly line forever. It was time to prove him dead wrong, baby!

About five years ago, during a transformative session with a life coach, a moment of clarity struck me like a light bulb illuminating a dark room. It was a profound question that emerged during this session: "What leads you to believe that you would excel as a probation supervisor?" This question demanded deep introspection, causing me to pause and reflect. In this contemplative pause, I recognized that my true sense of fulfillment was intertwined with my current role as a probation officer. The notion of becoming a probation supervisor, while tempting, wasn't aligned with my core identity—the caretaker within me that I had grown accustomed to.

However, me being me, my curiosity persisted. I decided to take one more shot at it, an attempt to pass the test and secure the role of a probation supervisor. Retirement loomed a couple of years ahead, and I wanted to eliminate the "what-if" that might linger in my thoughts. Unfortunately, my aspirations went unfulfilled, and the position remained out of reach.

Then, a significant turning point came during a breakthrough session with Forbes Riley, a life-changing encounter that served as the icing on the cake. On that pivotal day, the scattered pieces of my life's puzzle began to interlock. It was during this session that I unearthed a hidden burden I had been carrying all these years—the weight of a caretaker. This role had silently shaped my journey from a young age, as I instinctively embraced the nurturing qualities modeled by my parents and grandparents, perpetually shouldering the responsibility of supporting and caring for my family.

The passing of my father in 2000, after a tragic accident related to his struggle with detoxing from alcohol, left a profound impact on my psyche. I felt a deep sense of guilt and an insatiable desire to save others from the grip of addiction. Unbeknownst to me, this subconscious commitment to caregiving had become a barrier preventing me from embracing my own growth and self-empowerment.

Realizing this, I made a firm decision to break free from the chains that held me back. I understood that I couldn't continue to sacrifice my own dreams and aspirations in the name of caretaking alone. It was time to embark on a journey of self-empowerment, not only for myself but for all the women who found themselves in a similar predicament.

I came to a profound realization that loving myself first was not selfish, but an essential prerequisite for growth and fulfillment. How could I truly care for others if I neglected my own needs and desires? It was time to redefine my identity, to release the notion that my worth was solely tied to being a caretaker. I deserved to live a life that aligned with my passions and purpose.

With the support of my incredible husband of thirty years, who has always encouraged me to explore life to the fullest, I began to unravel the layers that had kept me stuck. I embraced the goodness within me, the strengths that lay dormant, waiting to be unleashed. It was a process of shedding the limiting beliefs that had been ingrained in me, replacing them with a newfound sense of self-belief and confidence.

Throughout my life, I had always been a source of encouragement and inspiration for others. From my elementary school years to college and my professional career, I had mentored and guided countless individuals.

Now, it was time to extend that same empowering energy to myself.

I recognized that women, in general, tend to take on the role of caretakers. We selflessly give our time, energy, and love to those around us, often neglecting our own needs in the process. It is a common pattern, one deeply ingrained in societal expectations and conditioning. But I firmly believe that we, as women, have the power to break free from these limitations and redefine our own narratives.

I encourage women to recognize the incredible strength and resilience they possess, the same qualities that make them exceptional caretakers. But I also implore them to redirect some of that nurturing energy back to themselves—to nurture their own dreams, passions, and personal growth.

Empowering women in the caretaker role is a transformative journey that demands actionable steps to bring about lasting change. Here's a roadmap to help you care for yourself so that you are not pouring from an empty cup.

Cultivating Self-Love and Prioritization:

- Dedicate time each day for self-care activities that rejuvenate your mind, body, and soul.
- Start a journal to track your feelings, accomplishments, and areas where you can improve self-love.
- Practice saying "no" to non-essential commitments to create space for your own well-being.

Setting Boundaries and Seeking Help:

- Identify situations where your boundaries have been breached and take steps to address them.
- Communicate your boundaries assertively, but kindly, to those around you.
- Seek support from family, friends, or professionals when feeling overwhelmed, without hesitation.

Creating Space for Aspirations:

- Create a vision board or digital space to visualize your dreams and aspirations.
- Set achievable goals that align with your passions, both within and outside your caretaker role.
- Allocate dedicated time each week to work on your aspirations, treating them as essential commitments.

Recognizing Your Right to Personal Growth:

- Educate yourself about personal development, attend workshops, and read empowering books. Like this one!
- Reflect on your personal growth journey periodically, celebrating milestones and learning from setbacks.
- Share your growth experiences with friends and family to inspire them to embrace their journeys, too.

Shifting Mindset and Redefining Self-Worth:

- Challenge negative thoughts by reframing them with positive affirmations.
- Practice gratitude daily to appreciate your inherent worth and uniqueness.
- Surround yourself with positive influences, such as role models and supportive peers.

Leading by Example:

- Model self-prioritization and self-love to those around you, showing them the value of these practices.
- Share your mindset transformation and inspire others to embark on their own self-discovery journeys.

Confronting Fears and Insecurities:

- Identify specific fears and insecurities that have hindered your personal growth.
- Seek therapy or counseling, if needed, to address deep-seated fears and work through them.
- Regularly engage in activities that challenge your comfort zone, gradually building your confidence.

Transforming Limiting Beliefs:

- List your limiting beliefs and counter them with empowering statements.

- Engage in positive self-talk and visualization exercises to reinforce your new beliefs.
- Connect with a supportive community or mentor/life coach who can help challenge and transform these beliefs.

Committing to Continuous Growth:

- Embrace a growth mindset, seeing challenges as opportunities for learning and improvement.
- Keep refining your self-care routines, boundaries, and aspirations as you evolve.
- Celebrate your progress and keep adapting your approach as you continue this empowering journey.

Remember, empowering ourselves in the caretaker role is a process, and it's essential to be patient and give yourself grace throughout. Your commitment to personal growth will not only uplift you but also inspire others to embark on their own transformative paths.

As caretakers, we have developed an innate ability to empathize and support others. So, as we learn or give ourselves permission to unleash our full potential, we must also seek out opportunities for personal and professional development. It may mean acquiring new skills, pursuing higher education, or exploring entrepreneurial ventures. We must let go of the notion that age or circumstances limit our ability to learn and grow. Every day is an opportunity for reinvention and discovery.

Perhaps, the most important aspect of this journey is cultivating a deep sense of self-love. It means embracing our flaws and imperfections, celebrating our strengths, and treating ourselves with kindness and compassion. It requires us to let go of self-judgment and comparison, recognizing that we are unique individuals on our own exceptional paths.

As we navigate this empowering journey, we must surround ourselves with a supportive community of like-minded individuals. Seek out mentors, join groups of women who are also on a path to self-empowerment, and celebrate each other's victories. Together, we can uplift and inspire one another to reach new heights.

Networking with other caretakers can also be empowering. Joining support groups, attending workshops, or connecting online can help you find community and support. You may also learn new strategies for balancing caretaking with personal growth.

Dear caretakers, it is time to unleash the extraordinary within us. Let us embark on this empowering adventure together, celebrating our strength, resilience, and unwavering love. The world needs us to shine our light brightly, for we are caretakers, empowered.

As a woman who has been a caretaker, I understand the struggles that come with feeling stuck and not growing to your full potential. It's easy to fall into the trap of putting others' needs before our own and neglecting our own personal growth. But it's essential to remember that our happiness and fulfillment matter just as much as anyone else's.

You may feel like your life revolves around the needs of others. Whether it's caring for children, elderly relatives, or a loved one with a chronic illness, your days may be filled with taking care of others' needs. While being a caretaker can be a fulfilling role, it's essential to remember that it doesn't have to define you.

If you're feeling stuck and not growing to your full potential, it's time to take a step back and evaluate your priorities. Are you neglecting your own needs, desires, and goals in favor of caring for others? If so, it's time to make a change.

It's also essential to communicate your needs and goals with the people around you. Talk to your loved ones about your aspirations, and ask for their support. It's possible that they may not even be aware of how you're feeling.

Finally, don't be afraid to pursue your passions and goals. Just because you're a caretaker doesn't mean you have to give up on your dreams. Whether it's starting a business, pursuing education, or exploring a new hobby, remember that you're capable of achieving your goals, no matter your circumstances.

In wrapping up this chapter, I want to emphasize that, as a woman and a caretaker, it's all too common to find ourselves caught in a cycle of stagnation, feeling as if our personal growth is hindered. However, the journey toward realizing our full potential is not an insurmountable challenge. It begins with the simple, yet profound, act of setting boundaries that honor our own needs and aspirations. Through clear communication and fostering connections with fellow caretakers, we create a network of support that can help us navigate the complexities of our roles.

Moreover, let's not forget the transformative power of pursuing our passions. By dedicating time to what truly ignites our spirits, we not only nourish our own souls but also set an inspiring example for those we care for. It's a journey that requires self-belief, determination, and a healthy dose of self-love.

Let this chapter serve as a starting point, a catalyst for your personal transformation. Embrace the journey ahead with open arms, knowing that you have the strength, resilience, and inherent power to become everything you desire. The time for self-empowerment is now. It's time to break free and step into the extraordinary life that awaits you.

WITH BRAVE WINGS, SHE FLIES

By Anna Cheney

I **BELIEVE WE ALL** have a story that will eventually bring us face-to-face with the calling of our life's work. Through a journey of unexpected interruptions in my life, I learned how to navigate my path without living in self-abandonment.

My calling began many years ago as a leader and mentor, which eventually brought me to a coaching practice. However, over the past seven years, I've faced numerous difficult circumstances that I refer to as "the storm".

I once thought I had a carefully-constructed life. Instead, these storms led me to years of self- abandonment and, eventually, into a thriving life of self-discovery.

Over the past seven years, I have faced several unexpected health challenges. In the midst of these, my husband, Doug, and I took in my aging and medically fragile parents to live with us. The first three months, we faced five 911 calls and six hospital stays between them. Through the post-traumatic stress filled nights, wondering what would happen next, we battled daily to help them maintain independence while keeping them from more emergencies. My dad fought congestive heart failure, kidney failure, COPD, and diabetes. Mom developed several lung diseases.

Our lives began to change, with numerous routines expanding. We dealt with medications being overseen, house details doubling, financial management, doctor appointments, and—of course—sleepless nights as we listened with our bedroom door open for any potential sounds of an imminent health crisis.

As the main caregiver 24/7 to my parents, there was no time for my own health concerns until I was forced to face a hip condition called avascular necrosis. Now I was met with my first joint replacement—yes, there were more to come, another hip and a total knee reconstruction done twice. While I was overwhelmed and needing some healing for myself, I chose to press on, insistent on putting others' needs before mine, feeling compelled to climb the success ladder in businesses and find some normalcy. I thought it was the answer to simply survive in this season of my life.

As I was recovering from my first total hip replacement surgery, my mom developed a life-threatening bacterial infection in her lungs. So, even though I was stressed out and feeling the pull to abandon myself for others, the old Anna didn't get any help. She settled into her codependency and people-pleasing lifestyle and, consequently, developed shingles from the stress of it all. More life-threatening illnesses for my parents continued, and just a year later, my second joint replacement was demanding attention. Unfortunately, the following year that same knee replacement failed, so a third surgery was necessary and added another interruption to my life.

Life is life, as I always say.

My husband's company underwent a management reconstruction, and he lost his job. Thankfully, reemployment happened within a few months, and we were able to move closer to our children and grandchildren. However, the pressure and physical strain on my body, soul, and mind during this time took yet another physical toll on me. I developed a pinched nerve in my neck, resulting in a challenging six-month recovery. At this point, my own physical needs still took second place after the care of others, especially in regard to my parents.

Yet, the storm of life continued on. My dad was overtaken by his vast illnesses—and Covid—resulting in his passing. During this time, my mom recovered from Covid and took a fall, which ended up requiring a total hip replacement. Shortly after both of those emergencies, she developed blood clots in her lungs, leading to pneumonia. Recovery was long and debilitating. Lastly during this two-year time span, my mom took another fall and fractured six ribs. As for me, instead of getting help so I could continue to help me, I chose to abandon my own needs and press on.

When would I wake up to what I was doing to myself? Instead of getting to the core issues I needed to face, my challenges drove me to avoidance. I became a master stuffer and stacker of the pain and suffering I was experiencing within my life. I had stuffed the problems so deep I began to not recognize myself. Full of physical pain, gaining 50 pounds, emotionally ready to cry or yell at any moment, I learned to stack the next priority onto my already overburdened shoulders and press forward, barely surviving.

Have you ever thought, "I just have to keep moving forward, and maybe it will get better soon"? Then you may be a master at stuffing and stacking, too.

As you may have guessed, I was really good at hiding what really was going on within me. It appeared, to those on the outside, that I had it all together. My career was a success. I made helping others look easy. I stayed connected to a world of friends and family. My motto and self-declaration were to always be "The Helper". Yet, over the years, it became evident that I was losing the battle—both inwardly and outwardly. I realized that my inner life was extremely stressful. I had no boundaries in place, and healthy habits were nonexistent. My whole being was keeping score, but I was losing. My carefully constructed facade was crumbling. The constant aches, pains, fractures, and other physical concerns were my body and soul begging for attention.

I was living a life-draining, joy-robbing, burdensome journey of self-abandonment!

Have you ever abandoned someone? Like really leaving them to self-destruct, completely turning your back on them? If that wasn't enough, you actually threw obstacles in their way to ensure they did not succeed! You belittled their value and often wished they would just not be in this world anymore.

I hear you yelling, "No!" That's exactly what I said to myself—until I realized that, in my pursuit to be all things to everyone, I had successfully and destructively abandoned myself!

The effects of my self-abandonment left me in such a state of overwhelm that the stuffing and stacking technique had lost its ability to sustain me. I emotionally retreated and mentally started living my life in a very dark box, suffocating.

For me, this was a survival technique because admitting that I was settling for "this is just how life is" was unbearable. To cope, I believed it was okay to play small as a daughter, wife, mother, nana, and businesswoman. And when I say living small, I mean truly living small—disconnecting, frustrated, feeling a lack of joy and happiness, not following my dreams and desires. Just showing up was how I kept life together. Then, I would retreat into my cozy box, safe from all the "asks" in my life. Because my life outside the box was full of "next"—chasing the next event, the next, "Yes, I can help you?" or "I'll meet that goal you set before me!".

The list goes on and on. But what I didn't realize is that the box wasn't really safe. I was dying—slowly—by abandoning myself emotionally, physically, spiritually, and mentally. There just wasn't enough time in the day to nurture my own self, so I abandoned the easiest person: Me! I continued to believe it was okay to settle for the comfort of the box.

But I was miserable. Trying to be all things to all people seemed like the right move, but was it? I told myself to just keep moving so I didn't have to feel the pain of lost dreams and the burden of heavy expectations. So, I pressed on, even as early in my life as when I was raising my children, being a queen of volunteering at their school and events, aspiring to be impactful in my community while aspiring to be a successful entrepreneur. There were days when

I thought it was acceptable to only survive with my nose above water. I'd tell myself at least I could breathe some air, because I, indeed, was alive. Or, so I convinced myself—most of the time.

While it may not seem like it, I fought back to live a more harmonious, fulfilling, and impactful life, to reclaim myself, proclaiming that I would no longer live in self-abandonment! I found if I could just get some air, see some light, and invite hope into my box, I could survive another day.

To survive meant breathing through the stress, going through the motions of my life, and entertaining negative self-talk, all of which made me feel I was suffocating. I'd grab my trusty ice pick and poke tiny holes in the box, believing this would give me sufficient air to breathe. It was a way for me to chip away at the walls that were enclosing me. It was the "fight back" when I got sick and tired of being sick and tired.

I had seasons where I had great success chipping away at the walls of my life. I'd have to say, though, it wasn't very hopeful since my tiny ice pick only had the ability to bring in a little bit of hope at a time—a little bit of air to breathe, a little bit of light to see the brighter side to free me from the darkness in my life. The only trouble with living so small is you think those itty-bitty holes are all you need to survive, barely living with your nose above the water.

I had hope many times and was imagining that I could run a business, be a mom, a nana, a caregiver, and a wife. I would hold onto that until another storm came my way and the cycle of retreat felt inviting again. I'd settle in, taking one step forward and three steps backward in my life *and* my business.

Sadly, I also took casualties along this ride with me. My husband, children, family, and friends were all affected by me "half" living for me, for them, and my business. I didn't realize how deeply it affected those around me until, one day, my daughter gave me a letter. It read:

Mom,

You are only one person. Try to remember that there will always be so many things that need to be done, but it's ok if it doesn't all happen sometimes. Please establish some healthy boundaries in your life, this will really help your stress level and exhaustion. Even if you just take one hour every day to completely relax, whether that's watching a Gilmore Girls episode, reading the Bible or a good book, going for a walk, or drinking a cup of tea on the back porch. I think you'll start to feel better. Being exhausted and completely drained day after day is no way to live. I pray you get some rest very soon.

Love, Krystal

This is one of most emotionally shocking letters I have ever read, and it was very humbling. My daughter was only 19 and devastatingly affected by the life I was living, the life I was role-modeling. My precious young daughter was watching me. I thought I was teaching her, and yet she was teaching me. My heart broke when I realized that I didn't need to be an alcoholic or drug addict for my daughter to feel responsible for my mental, spiritual, physical, and emotional health. She was trying to get my attention and rescue me from myself. As painful as this letter was, as have been a few since then, I thank God often that she wrote this to me.

By now you see the picture. I had settled in the life I was living in. And perhaps, you can live a long life of settling, allowing the circumstances of your life to choke out any chance of growth. But by allowing ourselves to live in an unpleasant situation, creating a life we feel we cannot escape from, we can lose ourselves—one thought and one choice at a time.

I mentioned being sick and tired of being sick and tired. When we have had enough, we make a choice. My choice to live a more abundant life took many, many years to make. I had to lay down my icepick and get out of the box to authentically thrive in my life and in my business.

Did I just walk out of the box? No! It took intention and purpose to find effective tools to free me from living the crazy cycle of my life, overloaded and consumed! It took bravery to admit to myself—and to you—where I'd been living. I think of this first step of vulnerability as telling the story of what's really going on in our lives.

Are you ready to be vulnerable with yourself and others? If your answer is a resounding *yes*, then let's get started.

I invite you to take a step back and look at where your life is going. Are you barely surviving? What would it take to have freedom from your box? Can you imagine living wholeheartedly with harmony in all aspects of your life?

Are you willing to say *yes* to finding a way to live for yourself and your loved ones? Are you ready to strap on brave wings and fly?

If so, your next step is to let go. You may need the support of others to walk this journey with you because this step is difficult. Then, you can choose to get into *empowered action*. For me, that step consisted of setting aside my limiting beliefs, finding hope, and bravely choosing to pick up a sledgehammer to knock down those walls that were entrapping me! What will your next steps look like?

For me, the key to breaking down my walls was tapping into several core strengths to stabilize my way of being. My first empowerment move was pursuing impactful relationships! Connection helped me snap out of the overwhelm, combat depression, and reaffirm my commitment to myself.

One step at a time, I acquired several more tools to empower myself in finding real freedom. Exercise, relaxation such as bubble baths and soothing music, scripture reading, or reading a book or listening to one on Audible would help me focus and bring awareness when I defaulted to white-knuckling my way through life again. I also became enlightened to my window of tolerance and stepped into grounding techniques, such as using my five senses in any given situation to bring me back to my full self. Another effective method of grounding is experiencing plain old dirt between your toes. Starting self-care can be as simple as a walk in the garden.

By now, you may be asking yourself, "Could it be this easy?". No, it's not easy. It's a journey, and, like mine, the awareness can take time, even years. But before you're back into the doom of life, overwhelmed by my sharing of the past seven years of my life as it was, I ask you to hear me out! The sledgehammer got me out of the box, and I lived! You, too, will need lifesaving tools.

Each tool has become my superpower. As I grew in awareness, I leveled up the foundation that I refer to as my five pillars, which build resilience within me. They were born from awareness of emotional intelligence. Finding training to attend, joining retreats to rejuvenate and empower me to live, hiring a coach, praying and finding my purpose by stepping into my life's calling, learning from coaches through their support and accountability, and learning the beauty of self-care and self-awareness were, in fact, not selfish acts. Rather, they became essential ways to appreciate myself so I could serve others with a full cup.

To set you up for inevitable success, I encourage you to take hold of these five pillars for stability and freedom! Build a life of resilience so you're not tempted to crawl back into the box of self-abandonment. Embrace relationships by finding a tribe that gives you the gift of connection.

Establish self-care routines and goals designed specifically for you. Learn to center yourself through powerful self-awareness practices such as journaling, breath work, and using your five senses to bring you into awareness. Astonishingly, these practices will connect your head to your heart.

Be intentional with your mindfulness. Approach your life with curiosity instead of judgment so that you can stay grounded in ever-unfolding moments and make compassionate space for what you're experiencing.

Run to your purpose. You know you have found it when you feel calm, peaceful, and just know you're doing the right thing. Be an explorer by stepping into your life's purpose. Be curious, sit down and reflect, take a personality test, try new things, and then go with what works.

Through my life experiences, I found the gift in it all. I found the longing and privilege to help others in truly living and thriving in their lives. Our experiences can lead us to finding the calling in our lives. As for me, I tested the waters with mentorship and moved into group coaching. Much to my excitement and surprise, I witnessed transformation, and that's when I decided to dig in even more.

Over the course of a year and a half of online schooling, I became a certified coach. I wanted more tools than just a sledgehammer to break people free. I knew transformation isn't a sudden change—it is taking lessons learned and letting go of past experiences to empower change. Transformation takes time, like a caterpillar's willingness to go into a cocoon and let go of its old identity so that it may, miraculously, become a butterfly.

Stability comes when we use all three legs of a stool. Support, accountability, and a system are all essential to staying true to who you want to be. Are you ready to live a life in beautiful harmony rather than a life filled with clanking symbols? It's possible to nurture your healthy self, emotionally, physically, mentally, and spiritually. Stepping into a life filled with powerful intentional steps strengthens us, during and through the storms of our lives.

Have you recognized yourself in this story? Do you resonate with a life of self-abandonment? You don't have to retreat to your box any longer. I'm right here—living proof that it can be done.

#togetherwearestronger

AWARENESS: YOUR FIRST STEP TO EMPOWERMENT

By Terri Mongait, EGC

*A*WARENESS! I WANT to introduce you to awareness. The definition of awareness is the ability to perceive, to feel, or to be conscious of events, objects, thoughts, emotions, or sensory patterns. We go through life completely unaware of many things going on around us.

So many things we take for granted because they are not in our immediate awareness. For instance, our toes and our teeth.

We really are not consciously aware of our toes or our teeth. That is, until something goes wrong! You get a blister on your baby toe—now you're aware that you have a toe, and dang, it hurts! Searing pain when you chew on the left side of your mouth—now you're aware you have teeth, and they are not working.

For me, awareness became profound in September 2009. And because of that awareness, I was able to empower myself to take control over how I responded to the messages I received through the course of my life, especially this most recent one. Let me explain. It was

September of 2009, and I was slowly waking up. Things seemed strange. The bed was smaller than my bed at home, and I had wires attached to me. I looked over to the corner of the room and saw my brother.

Wait, what?

My brother lived across the country from me, so what was going on here? Then I saw my husband—okay, that gave me a feeling of comfort, and everything seemed a bit better. On the other side of the room was a former colleague whom I had not seen in years.

This can't be right. What the heck is going on?

What I found out was that I was in the intensive care unit at LAC-USC Trauma Center and had been there for three weeks! I had sustained a TBI (traumatic brain injury), and I had a long road to recovery—three weeks in the ICU, in and out of a coma, four weeks in a rehab hospital, and four weeks in a transitional living center.

Peter, my husband, told me (not for the first time, apparently) that there had been an accident. I had come off my horse and been touch-and-go since. My first thoughts were, "Oh my gosh, that can't be right! Three weeks of my life gone. No, this must be a mistake. I'm fine. Get these tubes and wires off me. Let me go home. I want to see my dog. Peter, take me home."

Unfortunately, that was not an option. While I did not comprehend the severity of my injuries, I found out that during the past few weeks in the ICU, I had been in and out of consciousness (none of which I remember, which I would later learn is quite common). My incredible sister, Claudia, had been there with Peter and me for the first difficult week of medical decisions. Since she is a registered nurse, Claudia was able to help Peter understand the medical jargon, and she made sure I was cared for. She also kept me as dry as possible because, for a period of time, the doctors required me to be packed in ice to keep my temperature down.

One side of my head had been shaved, and a dime-sized hole had been made to put a probe in my skull to monitor my intracranial pressure (ICP). If the ICP exceeded a certain number, they would have to operate to relieve the pressure buildup on my brain. I am grateful to Spirit that I did not require surgery.

A few days into my stay at the transitional living center, I met with the director and chief neuropsychologist. He explained that before the brain injury, my brain function was at about a seven-eight (which is normal for a 52-year-old woman), but after the brain injury, I might be at a three-four. He cautioned that, after two years of rehabilitation, I might get back to a five-six.

I could have taken that diagnosis and added it to the messages I had accumulated over the course of my life. I could have accepted that I was not good enough, broken, and now always less than! Would I be able to continue partnering with my horses? I was still in my Equine Gestalt Certification classes. Could I graduate? Would I be able to start my business? Sadness, confusion, pity swept over me... all at the same time. And then, anger reared its head! Anger gave me kick in the pants I needed to change my immediate reaction into my own, chosen, response.

I returned to my room, and after some thought, I realized that I could *choose* how I responded to that message. I could empower myself to respond to the diagnosis instead of reacting to this trigger, like I had done all my life. For many of us, we have triggers that demand an automatic reaction. These reactions are due to the stories we have told ourselves and continue to tell ourselves over the course of our lives. But instead of automatically reacting to what the doctor had just told me, I chose to take a few minutes to evaluate the situation, and ultimately, I took control and decided to call bullshit on the doctor's diagnosis. Only I could put restraints on my recovery. I chose no restraints.

My recovery was tedious, something I found annoying. I had to endure physical therapy and occupational therapy every day. While I was still in the rehab hospital, I also had to work with a speech therapist to regain control of my swallowing reflex. After more than a week, I was finally "upgraded" to be able to use a straw and no longer had to drink a thick, nectar-like beverage for nutrition. Since I was now able to use a straw, Peter brought me my favorite Vanilla Bean Frappuccino to celebrate. I felt like I was finally on the road to recovery.

After enduring my recovery process and with the support of my husband, I moved my family to Colorado and started my business at Begin Again Ranch in Sedalia.

Today I'm an award-winning author, a successful business owner, and my passion is serving others.

My expertise lies in helping women and couples unravel their own stories. By partnering with my horses at my six-acre ranch, I work with the client, and—together— we determine the trigger, identify what the story is around that trigger, unpack the story box, and get to the initial message that actually wrote the story the client now carries around every day.

Horses are intimidating to many, as they are large, powerful, and somewhat unpredictable. This creates an opportunity for some to overcome fear and develop confidence. Working alongside a horse, in spite of those fears, creates confidence and provides wonderful insight when dealing with other intimidating and challenging situations in life. Like humans, horses are social animals with defined roles within their herds. They would rather be with their peers. They have distinct personalities, attitudes, and moods; an approach that works with one horse won't necessarily work with another. At times, they seem stubborn and defiant. And yet, if they are with a client, they are acting that way for a reason beneficial to the client. Horses provide vast opportunities for metaphorical learning, an effective technique when working with even the most challenging individuals or groups.

But even if you don't have a therapeutic horse nearby, I can help you along your healing journey. In order to begin unraveling your own stories, here are three steps to get started:

1) Choose to become aware of the stories you have been telling yourself over the course of your lifetime.

2) Become aware of your triggers that are holding you back/making you feel like you're broken/not good enough.

3) Start to *choose a more intentional response* by seeing that, maybe, you have to let go of who you think you are, so you can become who you actually are meant to be.

Now, we will break down this process further.

1) Awareness of our stories

Recognize that we all tell ourselves stories. But when did they start? Certainly not yesterday. Most likely they started years (or decades) ago. These messages are written on our personal whiteboard, over and over again, through the course of our life. And if you're familiar with using a whiteboard, the longer ink stays on the board, the more likely it is there will be a stain left when you erase it.

Early on in my life, I received the message that I was not good enough just as I was. I was around ten years old, and our family was on vacation at a lake in upstate New York. My older sister and her friend were going out on the lake with the boat. I wanted to go, too, but was not included. Luckily, I was pretty thrifty at that time, so I always had money saved (in other words, I didn't have many opportunities to spend my allowance). Suddenly, when I offered to buy either lunch or a tank of gas, I was welcomed to go on the boat trip. The message I received was that I was not good enough to be included just as myself, but I could buy my way onto the boat.

Years later, I was working with a client that had received similar messages over the course of her lifetime. We were in the arena with my herd of horses, and I asked her to make friends with one or more of the horses and have them join up and follow her. As she was interacting with the horses, I was coaching her to unravel her story of not being good enough to be accepted. The horses ignored her until she realized that she needed to accept and love herself first. As soon as she did, two of the horses approached her and followed her as she walked away. Horses mirror human body language, but more importantly, they respond to the client's energy.

Many clients complain, "This horse is stubborn" or "That horse doesn't like me". The lesson is that if the client takes the necessary steps to explore a different perspective, the horses will respond differently. Horses are honest, which makes them especially powerful messengers. So, when the client acknowledges their own story (and the energy around it), once they begin to observe the story from a new perspective, the horse will shift and respond differently, too.

Action step: What is the story that comes up for you that is keeping you from being the best you can be? You may be aware every time you speak with one of your siblings on the phone, you become anxious or agitated, and you're not sure why. What I want you to do is be curious and figure out what message is trying to get through to you. Starting today, I invite you to become more aware of these stories and journal about what that awareness is. You may not come to a conclusion yet, but starting the process will help begin to unravel your PTS (Post Traumatic Stories).

2) Triggers

Once you know your message/story, the next step is becoming aware of what triggers you, what makes you react. For example: You say to someone, "Wow, what an interesting color you're wearing."

Their trigger: When they were young, every time they dressed themself, their mom said, "Oh, what an awful color."

Message/story they heard: I have no fashion sense, I should stick to the same bland (i.e., safe) colors, no prints, etc...

So, the next time you feel you might have inadvertently triggered someone, you can say to yourself, "Hm, I wonder what her story is," and be more compassionate—unless, of course, their reaction triggers you. And if you are triggered, then become curious as to what your story is about the trigger.

As an example, one of my clients, Sharon, wanted to figure out why she kept sabotaging herself every time she got close to being successful in her business. I wanted to start with her definition of success (where/when did this story begin). She told me her father was very successful and ran his own company. What she remembers is that he never had time for family and all the family friends thought he was a complete jerk.

I said to her, "What I'm hearing you say is that being successful means you have to give up your family and be a complete jerk to everyone."

She sat back on her chair and said, "I never thought of it that way before."

As we were discussing this, one of the horses started trying to tip over her chair—he was being a real jerk! Once she had the realization that her idea of success was based on her father, the horse stopped bumping into her chair, let out a full body release, and walked off. Sharon realized that her definition of success was based on her father's story and did not have to be her story.

Action step: If you already know what your story might be, continue to explore more about the original message. Write in your journal and ask yourself, "Is that really true?"

For example, to be successful, does Sharon *really* have to give up her family and be a complete jerk?

To be happy, do you *really* have to do everything for everybody?

To be content, do you *really* have to give up your dreams and goals?

And finally, we have...

3) Intentional response

Empower yourself to overcome the story and choose to *respond* instead of reacting. Make the conscious choice to respond intentionally instead of succumbing to an automatic reaction.

Here, I share with you a client's experience changing from reaction to response while partnering with the horses.

I was working with Bernadette and Alan for couples coaching. On this particular day, they must have had a "discussion" in the car on the way to the ranch, as they were both clearly agitated when they arrived. We were seated in the arena, and I had Bodhi and Ki with us for their session. Bodhi is an American Quarter Horse and is my older herd member that is wise beyond his years. Ki is a Missouri Fox Trotter and is extremely empathetic and sensitive.

"So, what's going on?" I asked.

Alan started talking about what had happened in the car. As he talked, I noticed that Bernadette crossed her legs and her arms, then leaned over. I recognized a classic defensive posture. By this point, Alan was standing up and getting louder.

I sat there, contemplating how I would change their outcome. As Alan continued to try and get his point across, I knew this dynamic was a familiar one for them. I considered whether I should start with Alan and change his reaction of towering over Bernadette and getting louder to get his point across, thereby getting a different outcome, or if I should work with Bernadette to change her reaction of curling up, arms and legs crossed in front of her.

While I contemplated which way to go, Bodhi joined us, walked in between Bernadette and Alan, grabbed Bernadette's shoelaces, shook her foot, dropped it, and walked off. Bodhi changed Bernadette's posture and provided me with the perfect opening to coach them through the process of becoming aware of the event, their reactions, and what they had to do to change the usual outcome.

I turned toward Bernadette and asked her, "What just happened?"

She responded that Bodhi had shaken her foot and made her shift her focus. I pointed out that she had changed her posture as well. I coached her through Bodhi's lesson by asking her about her focus and posture before Bodhi shook her foot, and she responded that she was focused intently on what Alan was saying, which was something she always did whenever they were in the midst of a serious discussion.

"How else might your whole demeanor be interpreted?"

She looked at me, slightly perplexed. I knew she didn't recognize what I was pointing out. I said, "With you sitting there, legs and arms crossed, and leaning forward, might it give someone the impression that you are in a protective, defensive mode?"

She sat back, taking in what I had just pointed out. "Wow, I never thought of it that way before."

"How might you change your dynamic in these situations?" I prompted.

She thought about it a moment, did a whole-body shake, planted her feet on the ground, and placed her hands in her lap.

I turned to Alan. "Now how does that feel for you?"

"So much better," he answered.

I asked them to start again. Alan sat down, Bernadette sat across from him, open and receptive, and they were able to discuss the issue calmly, ultimately reaching an amicable conclusion. By changing their response, they were able to reach the outcome they both wanted.

Going forward, I invite you to explore the three steps I've shared with you to begin to empower yourself and unravel your own stories.

Remember to become *aware* of your stories, acknowledge your *triggers*, and choose to take a moment to *respond* to the trigger instead of reacting to it.

By reading my book, *Finding True Purpose: Life Beyond the Castle*, you can see how I was able to empower myself to overcome my own messages and obstacles, unravel my stories, and explore how they intertwined throughout the course of my life. I chose life, and you can, too. If you're in the Denver area, I invite you to send me an email (address provided in the About the Author section) so that we can connect at the ranch. And if you're not in the Denver area, please reach out to me anyway. Let's connect via Zoom and start unraveling the stories that are keeping you from living your true and most awesome life.

PART

2

LISTEN TO YOURSELF

*O*NCE YOU BEGIN noticing yourself, it becomes easier to actually listen to your inner chatter and the words that come out of your mouth. This second step in The Empowered Woman's Path addresses the way in which we self-sabotage, standing in the way of our own goals, success, and happiness. In the chapters that follow, the authors illustrate how—by listening to themselves—they came to the empowering realization that they were the only ones who could truly hold themselves back. The same goes for you.

Deanna Merlino and I connected in early 2022 through an online coaching program we were both in and quickly hit it off, since both our businesses focus on women's empowerment. I had the pleasure of being on her podcast, *EmpowereD with Deanna,* and have been inspired by her life and business story. In her chapter, she shares how her entrepreneurial journey unfolded as she navigated motherhood and the grief of loss. Deanna shares how she learned to trust and listen to her inner guidance.

I've known **Krista Garrett** virtually since January 2021, and besides our businesses, we share another passion: music. Naturally, her gentle and sensitive spirit comes through in her story and business as a musician, music teacher, and head of a music school. Her chapter amplifies the importance of finding and listening to our inner voice so we can express it verbally, in writing, or in music.

I met **Marti Statler** through one of my best friends when I started offering human design sessions. She was one of my first clients, and I felt drawn to her candidness and openness. In her chapter, you'll see what I mean: She holds nothing back, tells it like it is, and encourages you to tune into your intuition because it never steers you wrong.

I had the pleasure of mentoring **Marit Hudson** in 2021 after we connected in an online coaching program. I was so surprised and humbled when she reached out to work together, seeing as she is such an accomplished and successful individual. Her vulnerability shines through in her chapter as she confides in the reader about her self-sabotaging behaviors and how she's been able to find ways to go from being her own worst enemy to being her own best friend.

MAKING YOUR PAIN YOUR POWER

By Deanna Merlino

*J*UST A COUPLE years ago, my life looked a whole lot different. Given that timeline and everything that's happened between 2020 and 2023, I'm sure yours did, too. There is so much I could share about how I got where I am now, but let's start with when it all changed...

Honestly, I remember the moment perfectly. It was week three into the global Covid-19 pandemic, and I was having a full-blown dark night of the soul. Not sure what that is? I highly recommend a quick Google search because we all have at least one in our lives—sometimes many! But to keep it quick and simple, it was a *deep*, full-blown, depressive episode. And it felt as if the entire world was crumbling around me. Which, as you know, it really was. But I want to start with a little backstory to paint a full picture leading up to this moment before we can even think of fast-forwarding to after.

Let's start where it most makes sense. I was working a job in corporate America; I had a pretty great gig. I was the president of the company's right-hand woman. I did anything and everything he needed me to do. I wore a lot of hats and helped him make a lot of money. Truly, I was treated pretty well and received a lot of unexpected/ untraditional bonuses because of it—not a ton of money, but amazing experiences and opportunities that I am forever grateful for (think a free car and rides on his yacht with all my friends!). Twenty-four-year-old me loved this. And I was totally okay with it being that way, until I wasn't.

The job wasn't easy. It came with a lot of responsibility on my shoulders, enduring numerous angry workers on the daily, and I was the person they let it rip on at the front desk. That aspect made it certainly *not* worth the pay. So, slowly but surely, after enough days of coming home crying to my then-boyfriend that I just couldn't do it one more day, I knew I needed to figure something else out.

You see, I have no college degree. Up until this job, I had been bartending for about 5 years. I left that behind when I was really ready to settle down and truly wanted a legitimate chance at starting a marriage and family that would actually last (at this point I'd already called off one engagement). Not having a degree left me feeling as if I didn't have many options, but what I did have was the strong knack for interacting with people, an insane work ethic, and a built-in entrepreneurial spirit because I grew up with entrepreneurs as parents. So, when the opportunity "randomly" fell into my lap to become a network marketing professional (I don't believe in coincidences), with a head full of fear of failure and judgement from my peers, and my heart full of hope and a grand vision to live out my dream life, I jumped in without thinking twice. It was an opportunity for a career without a boss, one where I made my own schedule, and one where the sky was the limit when it came to my income.

I began to build it on the side, and not to my surprise, it didn't take long before this business was rapidly growing. Every day grew my confidence that maybe, just maybe, I could really make my big dreams come true.

One day, I had climbed up the network marketing ladder far enough that I felt safe to dream bigger than my reality had allowed me to up until that moment. I was living on personal development books, trainings, motivational speeches, and podcasts damn near around the clock. This newfound confidence pushed me to do the thing I feared most at the time: I asked for a raise. I went in prepared and had compiled my research and printed out what account managers, marketing/communications managers, and personal secretaries of a CEO made. Combined, it was a fantastic amount of money, which I wasn't making peanuts in comparison to. Terrified, I asked for a $5 hourly raise and got it without the blink of an eye. And then it hit me like a semi-truck—it wasn't actually about the money for me. I was hoping to be turned down, so I would have an excuse to leave. What did I do? I dug up the courage and decided to leave anyway.

Unfortunately, I found myself at another job that didn't fill my soul. Working in a male-dominated field, wearing steel-toe boots, khakis, and collared polos to work every day, selling construction tools and materials. How did I find myself here, you ask? Well, it offered almost double the pay and bonuses of my previous job. I thought, somehow, this money would satisfy the call for more. Again, I did very well. I was getting raises right off the bat, had awesome monthly bonuses and a long-term plan like a 401k, *and* was being flown to sales school for further training. I was proud, but this still wasn't it. If you guessed that I didn't last long there, you were right.

I had a sweet position as a private provider inside of a Tesla plant, and I had only one co-worker, my boss. The downfall? He was the *worst*. Not as a human—he was honestly kind. But he, too, was miserable with his life choices. And the amount of negativity that radiated off that man was literally making me ill. As this was before I had the slightest awareness about "vibes" and the clear fact that I am an empath, I didn't understand why it affected me so severely.

For the time, I kept cooking away at network marketing and personal development. At every presentation I hosted, I always said, "My goal is to, one day, fire my boss and be unemployable forever". One day, it clicked. Why couldn't I?

I really started to look at, and daydream about, what I truly wanted to do. I'd had the thought before but was too scared and self-doubting to pursue it further. However, thanks to the confidence and personal development I'd experienced in network marketing, I decided again to look at what it would take to become a personal trainer— something I actually really wanted to do.

I had been working out seriously for the past decade. I'd even successfully competed in seven fitness competitions up to the national level—so, I did the dang thing. I got my certification and sent out resumés to four local gyms, fearing the worst but hoping for the best. The next day, every one of them set up interviews, and I got offers from each gym! I took the offer as a group bootcamp-style fitness instructor. This was the first time my soul sang in a while because I was doing the thing I actually wanted to do! Everything was perfect until literally three weeks later, when Covid-19 hit.

I live in New York, so the gyms were shut down, and immediately, fear and panic set in. What had I done? I just given up a very well-paying job, bonuses, and a retirement plan. Talk about the beginning of a spiral. I'm sure some of you reading this can relate to having a similar experience during this tough time. I tried my best to enjoy the "time off" for the first time in my entire adult life, as I'd always been a hard worker. "Three weeks to slow the curve," I kept telling myself—until the news station announced the extension of the shutdown.

Now, we're back to the moment I mentioned earlier. Pair that with the rising death toll, the complete unknown, and—again—my lack of comprehension as to how sensitive of an empath I am, what could I do? Well, I cried. A lot. For days. I could barely peel myself off the couch to even go sleep in my bed some days. I had forgotten about food—not even to mention showering.

This went on until I realized a voice deep inside me was telling me I had to turn it around, that I *could* turn it around. I had the ability, and I had the tools. At this point, even though I didn't know much about running a business virtually, I decided to get comfy being uncomfy. And I started offering my opportunity for health, wellness, and income from home working online. Besides, what did people need most at this time? Remote work!

In turn, my network marketing business blew up, my team was expanding like wildfire, and so was the flame that had been slowly burning away at me from the inside out. And then it clicked: *This is it*. I can be an entrepreneur; I *should* be an entrepreneur. I answered the nudge and decided to jump all-in. I began offering personal training outside at the local high school football field until I grew enough word-of-mouth references and made enough money to become more legit. "By chance" (remember I don't believe in those), I found a full gym that had shut down but was renting out for what seemed like pennies and started offering private training sessions. This was my dream finally taking form, and I was here for it.

At this time, my husband and I had been struggling with unexplained infertility. Lo and behold, out of the blue after a year and half of trying and just starting the first steps of the IVF process, we were pregnant! As they say: On God's time, not your own.

I now had a new lease on life, a new reason for everything. I wanted to go as hard as I could, as fast as I could, before our little miracle got here. I expanded my knowledge and earned more certifications, and in taking all these aligned action steps, the intuitive hits for my next steps just kept coming. I decided to create my own personal training app to have the ability to offer my services to everyone needing guidance at the gym—or while stuck at home, considering it was now late fall of 2020, and the shutdown was still affecting many people.

In another "chance happening", I had made a post online about having terrible nightmares. What I didn't know was this post would start a conversation that would change my entire life. Someone I knew explained that nightmares can be a side effect of unhealed trauma. That's a story for another day, but I want to make it transparently clear that I had *a lot* of that, from traumatic childhood experiences, sexual assault in high school, to most of my adult life being spent in multiple physically abusive relationships. She told me that she was training with an energy healer that could help me. I had no idea what this even meant, but because I knew her, I was willing to give it a shot.

This healing changed my life. Everything I thought I knew about the world changed in an instant. It looked different. It felt different. And immediately, I knew that I was meant to live in a totally different way than I had been. Quite frankly, I realized that I was different. This healer also told me that our precious baby was also different, and that it was very important that we be prepared to raise a highly spiritually-gifted child.

For me, that was all I needed to hear. As with everything else I do, I cannon-balled into the world of energy healing and didn't come up for air. It's been scientifically proven that we pass our trauma on to our children, and I wanted to do everything in my power to heal every little thing I possibly could with what remaining time I had left.

Before we knew it, our beautiful and healthy baby boy was here, and nothing could possibly bring us down—or so I thought! My postpartum hit me like a wrecking ball. No one warned me about the 4th trimester, and I felt like I was lost at sea with no land in sight. I struggled, and I struggled hard.

Then, to make it so much worse, the unthinkable happened. My dad unexpectedly passed away three months later. To say I was devastated would be an understatement. The only thing that held me together were the beautiful hazel eyes of my son looking up at me for literal life support. And I thank God every day for what I have learned through energy work—that energy never dies, only changes form. I found some peace in the fact that, while I couldn't see my dad here in the physical anymore, he was still around somewhere out there, that he was still here with us, somehow.

Grief is funny. You grieve for what you lost but also for what they're missing out on. On one hand, my dad always wanted a grandson to build houses with and ride around in heavy machinery together. And on the other hand, my son will never get to grow up knowing the most incredible grandpa. But somehow, I know in my heart that they already know each other so well.

So then, at that point, I had a choice to make. Would I wallow in this heartbreak forever or use it as fuel to keep going? I think you know which path I chose. I decided to be the woman who would make my son proud—the woman who would make my dad proud. I dove as deep into energy healing as I could, and with my current 25 plus accredited modalities and tools, offer it to others via healing sessions and life/business coaching so others can live a soul-filling life as well. I started my podcast, *EmpowereD with Deanna Merlino*, after I received divine guidance from my father telling me it was time to share my voice with the world. I created an online training provider called the Empowered Academy, teaching energy healing so others can share this gift as well.

I dream that, together, we'll make this world a better place, one healed heart at a time. I also launched The Empowered Collective with my best friend since high school, who's on this same journey with me. Together, we offer in-person healing and abundance retreats and have an online healing and empowerment membership community. And my favorite part about this? I took over the business my dad left behind, and we host all our retreats right there on his land.

A little over 30 years ago, my dad built three massive, beautiful rental homes that he and my mother ran together as vacation properties. Thanks to this gift he left us, now my mom and I get the blessing of running the rentals together, while also healing together. There was once a time when I wanted absolutely nothing to do with running a business in that small town of Great Valley. Frankly, I was enraged when my parents moved me there my freshman year of high school. Ironically, now it's my favorite place to come back to. Now, I get to take what my dad built and continue his legacy in my own way, creating new and beautiful memories on the family land, in the homes he built by hand—with my mom, and with my best friend. It doesn't get much better than that.

You see, life is both painful and beautiful. And that's what makes it perfect. Without the pain, we'd never truly grasp the beauty. At the beginning of this year, I got the intuitive download that I would write a book and begin public speaking. I literally laughed it off, yet somehow, I knew what that meant. Less than six months later, here we are! I can promise we'll never know the how—it's not our job to. Trust God and the universe for that. Know that every single thing that has ever happened to you is being divinely orchestrated for your highest good. Even when you're in the trenches and it seems impossible to see that, trust and listen to your inner guidance. It will never steer you wrong. So, now I close our time together with this: It's your turn. Where can you make your pain your power?

FINDING YOUR VOICE

By Krista Garrett

ILENCE CAN BE deafening, isolating, but sometimes, also comforting. To someone with chronic depression, silence comes in disguise as a friend—a quiet companion that appears as a presence without judgment.

Don't be fooled. Silence is an enemy that creates a false narrative of security that isolates and divides without the necessary flags and warning labels that come with any toxic "relationship". What do I mean by this?

We are social creatures by nature. We seek out others for comfort, emotional support, and humor. We gather together to celebrate and mourn, and when the routine of going to social gatherings, work, school, etc. is removed, it makes us lonely.

I am, by nature, someone that thrives in my work, but I tend to be much more introverted. Given I work with people throughout the day and have students rotate as individuals and as groups, I can get mentally exhausted and find myself wishing for quiet. I find myself struggling to maintain balance, let alone sanity; thus, the hazards of having an advanced degree in psychology and being a musician come up. How do I remain emotionally healthy and available to my family while thriving in my much-loved passion as a teacher and musician *and* maintaining my need for mental quiet? How do I maintain more than the bare minimum standards when I need to be kind and listen to my needs on a physical, mental, emotional, and spiritual basis?

I didn't want to get up one recent morning. I have been told many times—and by many sources, I may add—that waking up at the same time every day, regardless of circumstance, helps one cope with stress and gives the person time to consciously decide how they will approach their day, albeit positive or negative. But on this morning, I didn't get up on time. I ignored the alarm.

I wasn't grateful; I wasn't thinking positively. I just laid there, wishing to stay put. I wanted, no I craved, to be left alone. With isolation, regardless of whether it has been mandated by outside forces or self-imposed, comes a loss of time, day, routine, and social interaction. In and of itself, that makes one question become a reality: What is real in life if what is around us is perceived from the inside out? If that is true, our situation and how we perceive and react to it is based on what we consciously believe. So, I could choose to believe that this situation sucks and that life as I know it is over and that I need to eat every donut in the Mid-Atlantic region and binge-watch the *Great British Baking Show* (don't judge me—for all you know, I'm just setting the scene).

As a matter of survival, individuals will create, almost involuntarily, a series of inner self-defense mechanisms that were evolutionarily used to help us in times of danger. When these mechanisms are used during times of threat, they serve us well. But in most recent times, these fight or flight tendencies have led those of us that are prone to depression, anxiety, and fear to be in a constant vigilant state. That can be exhausting, and it is a battle that can wear a woman down.

Once in this state of panic, the opposite tends to happen, and I will approach the situation with a self-imposed isolation that will often lead to depression, guilt, and twenty extra pounds of body weight. That doesn't have to be my reality. As much as I wish it away, there is a new "normal", and change, regardless of the source and reason, is threatening. So, in the face of change and threats, I find myself needing the inspiration to improve my mindset and become positive in difficult situations. What has become my magic elixir for dire times? Music.

The piano was my first instrument, my first love. As the oldest child of an Air Force family, we were selective with the activities we could partake in, given that my father could be transferred, and my parents wanted us to participate in extracurricular activities that could move with us. I started piano in Oklahoma City at the age of eight. I really enjoyed it, and it came easily to me. When we moved to Maryland, I dappled in flute during elementary school and continued piano lessons through my teens. I sang and loved to create harmony in the church choir and school chorus. My dream was to become a composer and concert pianist, but I would often struggle.

While my private teachers would tell me that I was doing well and excelled in technique and form, in my mind, my performance was always lacking. I felt inadequate. Psst... this is the part of the narrative where I share my "inner insight". I had a secret that I was afraid to share, but we will get to that in a bit. I studied music early in life, and it was difficult. I had to practice more than the other students and felt inadequate because of the internal self-analysis I would complete as I compared myself to my peers. Later, in high school, when we were in constant competition for performance opportunities and jury examinations with more critical evaluations that would destroy an already damaged ego, you could stick a fork in me. I was done!

For me, reading music was easy. But the technical aspects of playing were more complicated. I had inherited my mother's small, doll-like hands with short, dainty fingers. In piano, it is advantageous to have larger hands and long fingers to move quickly, have stamina, avoid strain in tendons in the hand and wrist, and play pieces by such great composers as Mozart, Chopin, and Rachmaninoff. At that time (the mid- to late-1980s), having small hands was a liability. I was told by a member of a prestigious conservatory that if I wanted to have the chance to be a concert pianist, I would need surgery to "elongate my hands" so that I would have at least an octave reach.

I have found myself staring at hands in later years, envious of long fingers that I knew could caress the piano keys with ease or coax beautiful strains from the violin or cello. It was recommended that I see a surgeon to have the area between my thumb and forefinger and the "webbing" between my fourth and fifth fingers sliced so that I would have the reach of at least eight notes. I must have been out of my mind because I actually considered it and went to a consultation. To think that I would be willing to mutilate myself, potentially losing all sensation in my hands from cut nerves and tissue, all to please the standards of others! It is a good thing that I am not a fan of sharp objects because, once I had a moment to think and develop some sense (and I'm a fraidy-cat), I quickly realized that would not be a good long-term solution.

I heard it all the time: "It is just in your head. There are other opportunities. You must need to work harder. There will be other opportunities". At the end of that process, I finally realized that I wasn't damaged, a failure, or worthless. I was depressed and anxious because, over time, my brain had changed its wiring to only entertain and process outside-in mindsets and influences. Given that this mindset development had taken place over an extended period of time, I needed to put in the effort and work consciously to stop the negative self-talk that perpetuated the negative feelings I had about myself. I'm not going to tell you that I don't have bad days and that all negative self-talk has disappeared, but little by little, day by day, it gets better with tools and dedicated work, and the good flows much more quickly.

When I use the word "work", I mean taking the time and opportunity to put in the effort to make changes within and around myself. What we have learned in recent years is that the brain is plastic. No, that doesn't mean your brain turns into a hard piece of matter, but rather that it is an electrical and chemical organ which can change, much like the shape of a muscle. It will be wired and communicate with itself based on what experiences, conscious thoughts, and exercises it is exposed to.

If it has been wired to react to negative events with fear-based reactions that last well after the perceived threat has passed, then that fear response will become the standard, whether there is actually something tangible to react to or not. The same can be said for feelings of peace and calm when presented with difficulties because you have conditioned your brain (over a period of time) to react and behave in a certain way. That becomes your "normal".

When something is not relatable, or we have no frame of reference for it, it is easy to dismiss it as an irrational reaction or make the excuse that the person is crazy. Well, I'm here to tell you, the reaction someone has to difficult situations, hormones, trauma, etc., is very real, biologically and emotionally, particularly to them and the people surrounding them. Think of it this way. Your brain (the third largest organ in your body, weighing in at three pounds of chemical and electrical impulses) runs the entire ship. If something is off with the captain, the ship will not steer or maneuver within its environment well. You can find yourself just circling, day after day with no course, unable to move past the negative, tired, unmotivated feelings that come with this cyclical thought process.

While reality is a personal creation (we each experience the environment around us differently), we can share what we surround ourselves with. Toxic breeds toxic, and positive breeds positive. For some, self-cutting becomes the release. It is a way for the person to redirect their attention and release internal pain, frustration, and self-loathing to an external source by creating an injury. When creating a wound, there is a release of energy. That energy has been repressed for a number of reasons, but regardless of the reason, it needs an outlet. For others, the outlet is self-medication in the forms of alcohol, drugs, or other addictions such as gambling and shopping. While there are a number of ways to create an unhealthy outlet to suppress hurt and pain, this doesn't have to be the path of least resistance. You, my friend, have the power of release through your words. Whether spoken or written, your words can set you free.

Get your journal, or if you are pressed for time and cannot access your journal, take a piece of paper and write. Get it all down on paper. Getting those words out of your head and into a physical, concrete form will remove the negativity, frustration, and hurt from your present being. Then I suggest that you take one of two options. The first option is to take the written thoughts and burn them, tear them up, flush them, and send them out into the universe, away from you. This exercise removes the power of the situation, the hurt, the anger from your brain, your body, your speech, and destroys it.

Want to use your words to find your power? The second possible option is to take those words and put them to music, either by singing or creating a spoken-word piece. Write a song that will express what you went through—or are going through—to remind you of what a warrior you are. This, too, is therapeutic. While your words express the trauma, you are dissociating the emotional power they have (or had) over you.

Not a writer? Pick up that iPad, tablet, or phone and voice record your thoughts. Then, the suggestion would be to listen to the recording once before deleting it. Or, again, use your words to create a song of your journey. The goal is to remove your conscious self from the situation, release the negative, and return to a place of peace, ease, and flow. This, then, becomes subconscious as you learn to act and be more solution-based rather than react by being fixated on the details of the situation when faced with self-imposed limitations and circumstantial challenges.

So, when you are tested, do you act or react? Let's visualize. You are walking along, minding your own business, and it happens. You are blindsided by someone, some circumstances that you were (or in most cases, weren't) prepared for. You are hurt, angry, frustrated, and discouraged. That feeling burns in your chest, your stomach, and your head starts to throb. You begin to question yourself, your circumstances, your spiritual beliefs. This could be short-term and fleeting, lasting a few moments before you are able to move on, or it could become an indelible thought—lasting many years.

Ask yourself again. When it is your season of test or challenge, do you act, or do you react? Are you absorbed in the problem's details, or do you go directly to searching for solutions? The choice you make will determine what amount of your mental, physical, emotional, and spiritual resources will be used. Will you find your voice to stretch and challenge beliefs and values to overcome your situation and circumstances, or will you become passive and just accept it as "it is what it is"? While I believe it's okay to challenge God, the universe, and yourself, what becomes a problem is when one becomes "stuck" within this well of negative emotions, fixated on the problems instead of the solutions.

There are always solutions; they just need to be imagined, dreamed, and found. In recent months, I have discovered this typically happens when I relax my thoughts and meditate during the day or listen to soft music while I sleep. I began this practice when pregnant with my twin daughters to relax my body (tense from constant brushes with early labor), and my mind while exposing the girls to music while in utero. My main focus, in my mind, was to help them grow and develop through stimulation and exposure to positive elements of the environment.

However, after pregnancy, I realized that this routine was actually very beneficial for my physical, mental, emotional, and spiritual being—and would later save me.

There was a span of four years where I was faced with depression, stress, and anxiety while creating a new business model as a music teacher/mental health advocate, transitioning into being a mother to not one but two babies (eventually three), and dealing with marital challenges, health challenges, death, and loss. When faced with all of this, I found myself not eating, with low energy, lethargic, and punishing myself because I thought I "deserved" everything that was happening to me. I accepted my circumstances as my new "normal" as a mother and a business owner. I felt isolated, depressed, and hopeless.

But there was light, and what I have come to realize with age (and beauty, I might add) is that I don't have to "accept" anything. I have a voice that, when used, can bring the resources, the people, and the opportunities I need. I am the author of my life; my reality is self-made. God pushes me daily to grow into the woman He intends to make an impact on the wonderous world He created. Thus, my point—are you someone that acts or someone that reacts?

In a time of uncertainty, fear, instability, you go ahead and be the cause and the effect within your microcosm. Know that you have the ability within you to create your reality. You can find happiness, create joy, find solutions, and realize dreams. The power has been given to you, so *use it*! Make the decision, today, this minute, to act. *Be the cause and effect in your life!* Not a sermon, just a thought. I know quite a few people that feel helpless, depressed, anxious, worthless, or plain tired, and they still do their best each day to put on a brave face. Just know that I know, I'm aware when it happens, and that I'm here and love you. You can do this. Know you are not alone on this journey, and the road you are traveling, while crowded, is full of support, understanding, and love.

YOU TRUST YOUR GUT. I'LL BRING THE COCKTAILS.

By Marti Statler

*W*HAT THE HELL am I doing?

I've asked myself this question plenty of times over the years. I bet you have, too. Have you ever been in that spot where you just knew things had to change? We all get there; it's part of growing and evolving.

I was at an impasse in my journey, with a knot in my stomach that only grew bigger over time. My status quo was making me physically ill. The thought of staying in the same place and doing the same things felt like life was being siphoned out of me. I hated being 'here', talking about the same topics, thinking the same thoughts, wishing the same things, and never getting over that hump that prevented me from reaching the place I wanted to be. It didn't matter how focused I was on the goal, how hard I hustled, or how much I had tried to manifest it— the hamster wheel was spinning and spinning with no end in sight.

But this time...

Enough was enough. I was done and ready to do things differently. It's not that I was "ready", per se, as I had been ready for a while. The object of my desire was always pulling me, and I thought I was moving toward it. The problem was I hadn't been taking the correct actions, the steps that would actually move me closer to the change I wanted. Looking back, my comfort zone was the issue. It had turned into a maze with no "exit" signs.

I would dream about what I desired and how it would happen. I could visualize it so clearly—the feeling of my surroundings, the touch of the plush, comfy chair I was lounging in, and the exact plants I had in my space. My stride was confident, backed by the kind of financial freedom that allowed me to make any decision needed and write checks to whomever, whenever. It felt fantastic! I thought all of this would come to fruition if I just kept working hard. But no matter how hard I worked, the progress was marginal.

Then, that day came. I was sick, grieving, and absolutely angry with myself. Why wasn't I good enough? I could never be good enough. In fact, this had been a core issue for me my entire life, but now it was getting in the way of my dreams. It prevented me from making the decisions needed to move forward. The minute someone would offer me a solution or an idea, especially if it was in direct opposition to the steps I knew I should be taking, I caved and backed out; because surely, someone... anyone... knew better than me.

Even though it was nauseating, my comfort zone was familiar and, well, comforting; it was a pain I knew and had overcome before. Anything outside of it was going to be a pain I hadn't yet experienced, and that was terrifying.

But growth doesn't happen when we're comfortable. It doesn't happen when the desire for the reward isn't greater than the fear of change. Growth doesn't start when change is fun and easy. It happens when there is a catalyst that sets things in motion. Mine? My dad died unexpectedly, pushing me into a gut-wrenching grief. Suddenly, the whole world took on a different shade.

I was sure that he would be the last man standing of his generation. We had talked about me caring for him in his old age. I promised that I wouldn't put him in a nursing home; when he could no longer wipe his own ass, we'd have to figure something else out—a Plan B. Now, how that compromise was going to look was yet to be determined because, even as a mom of three girls, my stomach is too weak when it comes to bodily fluids. Vomit? My hubby cleaned it up every time. I'd clean up the kids and he'd clean up the mess. Dirty diapers? Slobber? I wanted none of it.

One time, while driving on the highway, on my way home from work, I vomited all over myself. There was nowhere to pull over. I called my husband, who told me it was okay and that he'd clean the car when he got home. He's a godsend! Truly. My dad was aware of my weak stomach, so we'd laugh about how a mom could gag cleaning her own children's butts. It was a running joke that we would have to deal with it someday. So, when he passed unexpectedly, I felt my world stop.

Prior to his death, he had been asking me to stop by the house because he had something for me. I tend to live a full-throttle life and didn't make time to stop in. When I had gone to the house to be with Mom that first time after his passing, she went to the truck to give me the gift he had picked up. It was a slate painting of a red high heel with the words, "Life is Short, Buy the Shoes", on it. I lost it. The last thing he bought me was something communicating how short life is, and it was followed by his unexpected passing.

While we all know that life is short, and I can tell you that life is short, those words hadn't hit me until then. That realization vibrated through my whole being long after his death. I spent months thinking, crying, being angry, then drinking and thinking some more. The decisions that followed his death were not weighed against any logic, risk measure, or what-ifs because I didn't care anymore. It didn't matter if I succeeded, failed, went forward, or went backward. Life was short, and the shoes were waiting for me to buy them. I was tired of not doing what I knew in my gut to be the right choices for my life.

What did I really want? I wanted to start my own publishing company. I had so many ideas about what it would look like, who would get published, and how many women would read these stories. I wanted to affect change in their lives. I had been involved in publishing books for years, working under someone else's patronage. But while capable of running a company, there was always a subconscious excuse that prevented me from making moves toward that dream. It's hard to pinpoint what exactly that excuse was, since it didn't make logical sense. After all, I had written contracts, developed systems, interfaced with every author and every vendor. I managed the process, uploaded books, and created marketing plans. So, in theory, I knew all the steps. I just wasn't implementing them, at least not for myself, and simply continued to dream about how different all that would look if it were me calling the shots.

Everything we do has a cost. The longer I stayed stagnant, working for someone else, the more frustrated I became.

The time after dad's passing was a period of isolation. Grief pulled me back. It silenced me and turned my focus within. It had me questioning everything I thought I knew—and most of what I wasn't sure of. I have never been so rocked. While grieving Dad, reflecting, and getting angry, I had many epiphanies. One of them was that my commitment to helping others fulfill their dreams came at the expense of my own.

They say to find the silver lining in everything; if there was any positive outcome of my grieving, it was the lessons it taught me about myself. You cannot hear unless you are silent. You cannot connect with that which is in you if you don't make space for it. I didn't purposefully make space to connect with myself, but in his absence, I had no choice. This changed me. It was the kind of organic, unforced change that you cannot stop—nor would you want to. In that moment, and throughout all the moments that followed, I was a different Marti. I didn't realize the course-correcting decisions I was making, but none-the-less, they were happening and propelling me forward.

I didn't only switch lanes; I changed course. That course guided me toward my own desires, not the desires others had for me.

The notion that any decision is both seemingly insignificant and significant, capable of thrusting you in a new direction, is not lost on me. Given the number of choices we have to make, we could live a million different lives, none of which are inherently wrong. But every micro decision we have ever made has landed us right here... right now. Our life could still turn out in a million different ways, and likely will.

And as I reflect on my own journey here, right now, I'm able to recognize some of the choices that got me to this point. These breadcrumbs of my thought process give me an insightful look into myself, an awareness that allows me to both define who I am and redefine who I want to be.

You see, every achievement has a system behind it. It's a routine that, once perfected, can lead us to where we want to be. Many systems exist, and many more can be created; however, if one works for several of us, it will most likely work for others, as well.

My introspection led me to my system, the secret sauce, the formula to reaching my dreams. And if it worked for me, it could work for you. These were my steps.

1. Taking the Path to Self-Awareness

I had to gain the kind of self-awareness that allowed me to clearly define what I wanted and why I wanted it. I couldn't possibly have known these things if I didn't take the time to discover them. Unfortunately, my discovery was a by-product of my dad's passing. But being self-aware is transformational. Truly! No one knows us better than we do. However, it takes time to cultivate that knowing; it takes silence to hear our most inner voices telling us what we desire, independent of all the voices that have shaped us and all the responsibilities that have consumed us.

In 2020, after fourteen years of marriage, I took some time apart from my husband. Regardless of the reason for it, this break pushed me into a whole new territory. For the first time in my life, I was living alone. There was no one to care for, talk to, or cook for. I sat alone in my apartment, not knowing what I wanted to do, with absolutely nothing to occupy my time. What should happen? What's the next step in my journey? I had to figure it all out. And I did, by saying "yes" every time an idea popped in my head. I ate alone, traveled alone, tried new experiences, took long baths, and walked around my house naked. And it felt incredible! I realized that you don't know what you do or don't want until you try it all out.

As I said "yes" to new things, that new sense of enjoyment made me feel aligned—I was in the right place at the right time. It felt peaceful. I gained confidence. When I didn't feel aligned or peaceful, I knew that it wasn't for me. So, I didn't do it again. Not a big deal! But actually feeling the difference between what I liked and disliked caused me to recognize when my gut was trying to tell me something. And that is the crux of being self-aware; it's being connected to our intuition. We all have it. It always guides us to the right path. That gut feeling is our wisdom. She never steers us wrong.

This journey is not without challenges. Being self-aware demands vulnerability. If you can't and aren't willing to face yourself, your fears, your dreams, the lies you believe, and the truths you don't believe, you will not be able to connect with that part of yourself that propels you forward and toward all the glorious, untapped, delicious possibilities that are waiting for you. Full disclosure: You have to be willing to get real with yourself.

What does it look like to get real with yourself? That's what the next step is all about.

2. Embracing Bold Action

Learning to know myself and listening to my gut was only part of the process. It is so easy to know what to do. It is so easy to tell someone else what to do... but actually doing it? Sweet Jesus!

Once you get real with yourself about what needs to change, you can't stop there. Once I knew what to do, I had to be willing to act on it. It's worth repeating. Knowing and doing are two very different things. There are things right now, as I sit and write this, that I know I should do but I'm not doing. Some of them aren't happening because I'm not ready to expend the energy. Honestly, it's still pretty scary. Some of them are lies I'm still telling myself. But this is part of being self-aware—knowing what you should be doing, why you're not doing it, and owning it.

I don't know what getting real with yourself means for you. I don't know your why nor your solution. But for me, it started with taking a hard look at what was going on intrinsically (in my soul, body, and mind), why it was that way, and then committing to doing the hard shit. It became a lifestyle, a part of my daily routine. The exact method and outcome looked different every time.

For example, I remember the time I needed to pull myself out of a financial hole. After a deep introspection into what got me there and why, I decided to do things differently. So, I got a second job, bartending and closing up shop most nights. The very next day, I was at the bank making a deposit. Budgeting became my new talent. I stopped spending money on hair and makeup. Listen, that was rough for me. Good quality makeup and hair dye were a regular investment in myself. But for a year after I ran out of makeup, I didn't buy more. I also didn't do anything with my hair outside of ponytails and top knots. Looking like a hot mess was the price I needed to pay to reach my goals. That was me getting real with myself. I wanted to pay off debt more than anything else; so, I had to see where my money was going, where I could cut costs, and how I could bring in more money. And it paid off!

Another time that I had to get real with myself, and this was one of the toughest situations to implement my system in, was when I had to take a hard look at my shortcomings in my marriage. I frequently assessed what was going on inside of me before I verbalized it to my husband. It involved curbing my urge to let insults escape my lips and, instead, offering an "I'm sorry. What can I do differently?". This is not easy when it's not your knee-jerk reaction.

But action... action is the medicine that moves you forward. By far, the boldest action I have taken was working for myself. If there is an issue, there's no one else to look at for answers outside myself. The buck stops with me. I steer the ship. But that's what visionaries and dreamers do. And they get the reward with the risk. Remove the satisfaction of helping someone get their book done, remove the pride in having a book look amazing, give no thought to the flexible schedules and working with amazing people, and I am unfulfilled. And unfulfillment is the crux of those who sit and do the same thing, day in and day out. It's for those who talk about the same thing, who dream the same thing, who hope for better, forgetting that action is the medicine that will move them forward.

If you are unfulfilled in any area of your life, you *must* take action. You have to do something different. Staying in your rut is like poison to your soul. Stagnant water breeds disease.

When I had my come-to-Jesus moment after my dad died, wondering what I was doing with my life, my medicine—aka action—was starting my business. I was ready for the challenge. I had to be because I was so sick and tired of being sick and tired.

The scariest part of making these decisions was making them publicly. You don't have a business if you don't have clients. But in order to get clients, you have to tell people what you're doing. When I got my first client, I had no website, no business card, and no business email—all things I thought you had to have before that first client would take you seriously. Dianne's, one of my first mentors, voice was ringing in my ear, telling me to get comfortable with being uncomfortable. To this day, I remind myself of that. It was back in my insurance days. What Dianne knew, and what I came to find out all those years ago, is that bold action will require you to make moves so scary you want to throw up. And the very first time I convinced myself to get comfortable with being uncomfortable was when I had to make my first cold call.

My first cold call in my insurance days... shew! I circled around the business I planned to visit, probably ten times, smoked a few cigarettes, went through a car wash, and then went in. I made an appointment with the business owner and ran out of there as soon as the date was set.

He probably knew I was freaking out inside. In fact, I didn't even tell him my company or the reason for the appointment. At least I didn't throw up.

The first of anything new is always the hardest, and it always gets easier from there. Always.

I know there is action that feels too big and, absolutely, too scary. Start small. Lots of information is free, though sometimes you need to sift through it to determine what is legitimate. But start by getting information. You cannot make a good decision without it. Take that baby step. I have found that, as long as I'm moving outside my comfort zone, I'm progressing, growing, and learning. And when you continue taking action despite uncertainty, risk-taking becomes a natural part of the journey; so, that knot in your gut gets smaller. Does it ever go away? Nope. Not for me, anyway. Every time I do something new, it's scary. But I know that now, and I've embraced it as part of my process.

3. Finding the Power of Trusting Yourself

Trusting yourself is what happens when self-awareness and bold action intersect. The noise from others' opinions gets replaced by confidence. It frees us from the burden of others' validation. Does it feel nice to have validation? Of course. Do we need a support system? Absolutely. But do we need validation from someone who is not making our decisions or paying our bills? No. No. And no. When I make decisions based on what my gut has already told me, that's the end of it. I just know what to do and go for it.

When my dad died, I was forced to slow down, which is a nice way of saying that I couldn't function. It was a rock-bottom, of sorts. I made some quite big decisions in this time frame, with zero regrets around them. Making these decisions required me to trust myself. I had to have an unwavering belief in myself and my abilities. No, "unwavering" is not the best word to use because I absolutely wavered. In fact, "have" is the wrong word. I had to find that belief, a point reached at the end of all the winding doubt.

Make no mistake. Trusting yourself is not a constant; it's a fragile and, sometimes, elusive milestone. But it all comes back to determination.

I stayed the course. I asked myself a hundred and fifty-three times if I could do what I was setting out to do. And while I had no idea what the end result would look like or how I was going to get there, I was going for it anyway. Trusting myself means prioritizing myself. When I relax and get quiet, when I hear, listen to, and feel that gut instinct, the information flows. In fact, I make space for it.

Most of the time, it's at the beach. My favorite spot in the world is right beside the ocean. I swear, it feels like the sand is ready to absorb every bit of stress from my body the minute my feet hit it. I lay beside the ocean as the roar of the water envelops me; every cell calms down. When I am there and quiet, when the peace permeates my being, I am more in tune with myself, with nature, and with my gut instinct that has never steered me wrong. In that moment, my intuition takes over. She tells me exactly what I need to do, at first in the form of a powerful inkling. But eventually, that feeling turns into a full-blown plan which I can trust because I've allowed myself to do so before and been successful with it.

A couple of years ago, I hit an obstacle in my business, and I didn't see a way out. I didn't know what to do. Although, I actually did know but wasn't making space to hear it. Caught up in the noise, the right decision was escaping me. As I was driving to the beach, new book ideas were popping out. This was odd. I was contemplating quitting on my business; where in the world did new book ideas come from? But I let it play out. On my way to the beach, with a notebook, a pen, and a beverage, it all began to connect. It took a whole thirty minutes for me to get the exact plan on how I was going to continue with my business. Quitting was never really an option. It was victim Marti thinking about the easy way out. CEO Marti said, "I'll chew glass shards before I quit." I needed to stop, take a break, change my environment, and listen to my gut. She already knew what to do. I just had to listen.

Trusting yourself becomes a matter of following your intuition without second-guessing or questioning yourself. Right now, there is probably something you need to decide on. I don't care what it is; just ask yourself the question and listen. When my girls and I are discussing decisions that need to be made, I do this exercise with them. If they are struggling, I reflect back on the question they are struggling with. One of my daughters had a job offer that came out of the blue. The money was great but would require travel. Could she figure it out with kids? Yes. But she was struggling with what to do.

Here's how that conversation went:

"Linz, stop. I'm going to ask this question, and I don't want you to think about your answer. Just blurt out the first thing that comes to you. Ready?"

"Yes."

"Should you take this job?"

"No. But..."

"No but's. That's your answer. Stop trying to logic your way through it."

She didn't take the job. And she didn't regret it. The reasons became evident after the pressure of the decision was taken off her shoulders.

If you're trying to figure out what to do, try this exercise. If you can't do it for yourself and don't have someone to do this with, email me.

Ask yourself the question and listen to that very first answer. Don't think about it. Don't process why it's a good idea or a bad idea. It doesn't matter. Just listen to your answer. If it doesn't work out the way you hoped it would, it's fine. Make a new decision. Nothing says a decision is forever. It's not a sword to die on. Choose again... and again, if you need to. My daughter is getting ready to take a travel job, and now it is the right decision.

Embracing trust in ourselves reveals our potential. We are capable of creating our desires and dreams without relying on others. We have access to all the tools, all the resources, all the knowledge we will ever need... within us. Our intuition is always right. She never steers us wrong. Trust that.

And trust me when I say that being empowered is not about a singular moment in time. It's a way of life. It's embracing your CEO-ness with every ounce of unwavering confidence in your body.

Every woman can choose to live empowered, and the process to get there lies in knowing who you are and trusting your own compass. I can tell you how I've embraced it. I can give you some bowling bumpers to find your own path. I can tell you how intuition feels in my body and give you tips on how to feel yours. But I can't do the work for you. Wherever you're stuck, you already know your answer. You, my friend, have to take the bold action that you know you need to take. And you, my friend, are more than capable of doing the thing you really want to do.

I'd love for you to drop me an email and tell me what action you're taking next. I'll be your business bestie, your encourager, your ass-kicker. You'll never find a negative Nancy, know-it-all Karen, or dream-crushin' Deb in me. There's room for all of us at my table. I'll bring the cocktails.

FEARFUL TO FEARLESS

By Marit Hudson

"YOU ARE NOT intelligent or connected enough to succeed in a career in law," whispered the voice inside my 18-year-old mind, the voice I now call Ms. Fearful. She hurt me by saying this. I needed her support, but she seemed to think I was deluding myself. I gave more consideration to my dream of becoming a lawyer. No one in my family had ever studied law, become a lawyer, or knew much about law, so what made me think I could do it? Was Ms. Fearful right? She repeated herself intermittently throughout the day.

"You know you've bitten off more than you can chew this time—you don't have what it takes to complete an MBA." My head was spinning from the accounting module that kicked off my MBA. Again, I needed Ms. Fearful's support, but she wanted me to quit. I wondered if I, personally, knew anyone who had completed an MBA. Did I know what it took? Should I be listening to Ms. Fearful? She kept repeating all the reasons I would fail.

"Moving to a foreign country, alone, without any contacts, is a crazy idea. You may not make it work. Lots of immigrants fail. I hope you know what you are doing." Ms.

Fearful was there again, making me doubt myself. What if I didn't make it in a new country? I had a lot to lose. Maybe I was being too ambitious.

Ms. Fearful could be exhausting at times, frequently telling me I wasn't good enough, or alternatively that I was "too much" of something, both of which translated into doubting if I would be successful. What made it worse was that I didn't understand the reason for Ms. Fearful's whispers or how to deal with her. Would she always be there? Did anyone else have a Ms. Fearful? Was there a way I could manage her? Taking all these questions into account, I came to realize that Ms. Fearful actually provided me with a golden opportunity—learning how to manage and transform her, and in fact, enjoy proving her wrong! She was a gift.

Although Ms. Fearful had good intentions at heart because she wanted to protect me, I didn't need her to hold me back. I chose to transform Ms. Fearful into Ms. Fearless and believe I was enough, that I'd always been enough and would always be enough. Contrary to what Ms. Fearful told me, I became a lawyer (now with over 20 years' experience, predominately in a foreign jurisdiction), I singlehandedly moved to and lived in two foreign countries in my adult life, I got my MBA, and then I competed four times as an amateur bikini bodybuilding athlete in the National Physique Committee, the largest amateur bodybuilding organization in the US. However, these are just external achievements. The real win I want to share is the confidence I have gained by being stronger than my self-doubts, self-criticisms, and chronic overthinking. I coached my Ms. Fearful into becoming

Ms. Fearless, and I still do it whenever I face challenges or obstacles.

This chapter is for anyone who struggles with self-sabotaging thoughts because I am living proof they can be beaten with self-awareness, compassion, and discipline. In this chapter, I will share some key information and immediately implementable actions to help you manage self-doubt and overthinking so that you are no longer fearful and/or living anything less than the best version of your life. The following sections contain an explanation of each concept and then a practical and easy way of implementing the teachings. Enjoy uncaging yourself from your own mind and reaching new levels of confidence!

BECOMING THE OBSERVER, NOT THE PARTICIPANT

> "Thought is not reality; yet it is through that thought that our realities are created"[2]
>
> —*Sydney Banks.*

I've learned that thoughts are just thoughts—they come and go like clouds in the sky. They are not facts, nor are they reality. We have millions of thoughts, and some are more recurrent than others. The more recurrent a thought

---

[2]   Banks, Sydney. AZ Quotes. Accessed September 12, 2023. https://www.azquotes.com/quote/807864.

is, the more embedded within our psyche it becomes, like a path through a forest—the more times the path is travelled, the more deeply imprinted it becomes.

Our ego will tell us thoughts all day to keep us safe. An example of a healthy thought coming from the ego might be, "don't drive too fast on the freeway because you could crash". We know that we must stick to certain rules and boundaries, so our behavior doesn't endanger us. However, the ego will also send us a ton of unhelpful thoughts, such as "don't speak in front of that room of people if you don't want to look foolish" or "don't ask that person to go for coffee because they will reject you". Again, the ego has the best of intentions; it wants to keep us safe and free from harm, but these defense mechanisms can keep us stuck because we become unwilling to act in any way that might make us feel uncomfortable. When it comes to wanting to be the best version of yourself, both personally and professionally, feeling uncomfortable is inevitable because growth requires new challenges and adventures.

So, what's the solution? A key turning point for me was when I reframed the way I experienced these thoughts. Rather than viewing them as always reliable, true, and requiring action or inaction, I learned to listen to them as an "observer" rather than an active participant. When I learned to be the observer of my thoughts, accepting that they were trying to help me by keeping me safe, I stopped assuming they were facts. The game changed for me. I was able to speak to myself and give myself reassurance that I knew my thoughts were trying to help me, but I was good with taking calculated risks because I believed in myself, organized myself, and was willing to do the work.

Once I got into the practice of observing my thoughts, I empowered myself by not only noticing my thoughts but choosing to replace them with more supportive ones. By choosing to embrace empowering and supportive thoughts instead of giving attention to thoughts that do not serve you, you allow yourself to create the reality you desire.

An example of this is as follows:

Thought – "You won't be able to do this. You aren't intelligent enough."

Me, as the observer – "Thank you for sharing this with me, but I know I can do this because I believe in myself. I've done difficult things like this before. I have a plan, and I'll do the work to make it happen."

I'm not, for one moment, saying that doing this once will change the way you think because it is a practice that needs to be cultivated with discipline. Your ego that produces these self-limiting thoughts is not going anywhere, so rather than listen to it without question or seek to resist it, begin to speak to yourself lovingly, thank the thought for trying to help you, then reassure yourself you don't need this type of protection. By adopting this mindful practice on a frequent basis, these thoughts will be managed far more easily and in a healthy way that will empower you to feel more confident and excited.

Getting into a habit of viewing your thoughts as separate from "you" as an observer and reframing them—and even thanking them—will dampen your fears and increase your confidence.

RECONNECTING MY MIND TO MY BODY

> "After feeling disconnected for so long my mind and body are finally coming back together."[3]
>
> – *Rupi Kaur*

We often say that the body and mind are indisputably connected, but I know many of us, including myself, subconsciously disconnect the two so that we dissociate from our bodies and live in our heads. This becomes a coping mechanism when it is too much to feel the emotions in our bodies. For overthinkers, the coping mechanism becomes trying to "think" ourselves out of uncomfortable feelings. Of course, this tendency can sometimes be beneficial. For example, when we need to dampen the emotions we feel while doing something difficult, like not wanting to go to the gym but pressing on anyway because we tell ourselves we should, it is useful. It can also help us maintain a level of disconnection when we need to complete a certain task in a pressurized environment. I know it has helped me in business when logic needs to prevail over emotions.

However, living in our heads for too long with a sense of disconnection from our bodies can be unhealthy because we fail to "feel" our emotions at all, tricking ourselves

---

[3] Kaur, Rupi. "Home Body Quotes and Poetry." Scribble Whatever. Accessed September 12, 2023. https://www.scribblewhatever.com/home-body-quotes-and-poetry/.

into the false belief that we can "outthink" our emotions. Our minds work overtime, and the energy in our bodies becomes stuck. We don't heal from emotional distress in a healthy way. In a best-case scenario, we suffer emotional paralysis due to the over-analysis in our heads, and ironically, our thoughts become more muddled and lack clarity. In the worst-case scenario, we are left exhausted, burned out, and depressed.

What's the solution? How do we keep our minds and bodies connected so we are firing on all cylinders and being our best selves? We need to get back into our bodies and allow our energy to flow again. This means moving, dancing, walking, running—whatever feels good for you! I learned that lifting weights, connection to nature, walking, and running take the focus from my mind to my body and give my mind a much-needed rest. Not only do I feel more connected and calmer when I move, but I have a sense of mental clarity where my thoughts provide creative and positive solutions to problems I would previously overthink. If overthinking is an issue for you, or you just feel stuck in your thoughts, try implementing daily movement as a discipline and see how much better you feel—even after one week.

Daily movement will reconnect your body to your mind, reduce pointless overthinking, and cultivate a new level of peace and clarity.

BECOMING MY OWN BEST FRIEND

> "The most important relationship in your life is the relationship you have with yourself. Because no matter what happens, you will always be with yourself."[4]
>
> – *Diane Von Furstenberg*

I'm sure you've heard before the saying that if you spoke to your friends the way you speak to yourself, you'd have no friends. I know for sure I've self-bullied, belittled, and berated many times without even being conscious of it. Once I became conscious of the power of the words I would say to myself, I became intentional about speaking to myself in a loving and empowering way.

You can still be accountable to yourself for your actions, but rather than judging yourself harshly about every perceived failure, you can practice speaking to yourself as you would a friend in the same circumstances. Understand that negative thoughts and feelings will come up because you are human, but you get to *choose* which thoughts you pay attention to. Rather than live in denial about these negative thoughts, which can be unhealthy, accept that they come up because you are a human being, and all human beings who care about achieving

---

4   Von Furstenberg, Diane. "Diane Von Furstenberg > Quotes > Quotable Quote." Goodreads. Accessed September 12, 2023. https://www.goodreads.com/quotes/278144-the-most-important-relationship-in-your-life-is-the-relationship.

something that is difficult will have moments of self-doubt and uncertainty.

Getting into the practice of speaking to yourself in a kind and encouraging manner will change your energy and raise your confidence. It sets the tone for what you will and won't accept from the mouths of other people. One way to get this habit rolling is by speaking to yourself in the mirror and telling yourself you love and cherish yourself. Another practice is journaling positive and empowering affirmations, which can counteract words of self-doubt you may have floating in your head. You can even thank your negative thoughts for shining a light on where you could use a little more self-love and appreciation. For every negative thought that comes up, choose three empowering statements to counterbalance it.

For example, the negative thought might be, "I'm not sure if I'm good enough to [insert whatever dream you have your heart set upon]". The empowering statements you choose (which you can say out loud or journal) might be, "I am worthy and capable of making my dreams come true", "I can deal with any obstacles that stand in my way", and "With preparation and practice, I am not only enough, but I am *more* than enough".

Building a practice of speaking to yourself (even silently) in a positive and compassionate way will increase not only your happiness but also your levels of growth and success.

HOW CAN I SERVE?

> "The best way to find yourself is to lose yourself in the service of others."[5]
>
> — *Mahatma Gandhi*

I'm sure you will agree that lots of overthinking can come from contemplating what you did or did not do right and/or also whether you are not enough or too much of something. It is all about the self and ego-based. One of the major things that has helped me get past these difficult cycles is asking myself "how can I serve right now?" and then focusing on doing whatever that is. This can help move the focus from overanalyzing to getting really clear on what you can do in the present moment to serve others around you—or the world at large.

Sometimes, service in the present moment can be listening intently to someone so you can understand what they are saying rather than listening merely to reply. Sometimes, it can mean smiling at a stranger in the street rather than putting your head down and walking past. Sometimes, it can mean being entirely present for someone, entertaining someone, hugging someone—

---

[5] Gandhi, Mahatma. ""The Best Way to Find Yourself Is to Lose Yourself in the Service of Others."–Mahatma Gandhi." Medium. Daily Reflections!, April 6, 2023. https://medium.com/@officialprpatel002/the-best-way-to-find-yourself-is-to-lose-yourself-in-the-service-of-others-mahatma-gandhi-446d16c13385.

it can have a multitude of meanings depending on the circumstances of any given situation.

Service can also become part of your everyday life if you find a specific community, cause, or passion that you want to give your energy to. I have, personally, found that being a mentor/coach for younger women who are likely to go through similar challenges and fears—both professionally and personally—has been particularly rewarding. I get to channel my energy into helping others make positive changes and grow to their full potential. Imagine the younger version of you and what she needed. Now, be that to someone else and watch how the focus on any doubts about your own capabilities simply melt away.

Service to others, either spontaneously in the present moment or as part of a planned regular activity to a cause you are passionate about, will dramatically increase your confidence in yourself.

I hope you have enjoyed this chapter and that it has shifted your energy, even slightly, away from being fearful and closer to being fearless. Even knowing that negative thoughts happen to everyone can be freeing. Knowing that you can consistently manage your own thoughts is empowering and one of the most worthwhile ways of increasing your confidence, growth, and overall happiness. You become free to be everything you are supposed to be.

Be sure to read my bio in the back of the book to get access to a free eBook that can help you along your path!

PART

3

FORGIVE YOURSELF

I **ALWAYS SAY THIS** is the midway step for a reason: It could be the most important one. It's almost like getting over the highest hump in your path to come out on the other side. After overcoming this big peak, the downhill journey goes a lot more smoothly because self-forgiveness must come before self-empowerment. Once we take the time to notice and listen to ourselves, things we unconsciously or consciously chose to ignore come to light. Then comes the urge to beat ourselves up, and as I mention in my first book, "Your eyes are opened to your challenges, but you can choose to embrace and love yourself through those imperfections"[6] (p. 33).

---

[6]   Spirk, Marta. 2021. *The Empowered Woman: The Ultimate Roadmap to Business Success*. Mom Does It All LLC. https://www.amazon.com/Empowered-Woman-Ultimate-Roadmap-Business/dp/B09PHBST2T.

This is what this section is all about, and in the chapters that follow, you will see the common thread of forgiveness weaved through each story as these women find ways to accept their perceived failures, guilt, and shame as learning experiences to empower themselves.

I've been connected with **Barbara Conway** virtually for quite some time, but it wasn't until early 2023 that we got closer. Her story of resilience and fun-loving personality have a way of making a mark, and I'm blessed that she shared in her chapter how she's forgiven herself, others, and circumstances to carve her path into entrepreneurship and build a non-profit while working full-time.

I had the pleasure of meeting **Bella Bliss** in-person in September 2022 after knowing her for over a year when she joined my membership, The Empowered Woman School. Her name does justice to her energy, which says a lot considering all she's gone through in her life. In the next few pages, you'll get to follow along her journey of empowerment by watching her learn to extend forgiveness to herself and deciding to guide others to do the same.

Paris Byrum was another woman I met through other contributors to this book (Anna Cheney and Vesta Hager). I was impressed by Paris right off the bat, as she was the last one to join this collaboration and challenged herself to write the chapter even before we began the project—that's how much of a doer she is. Her chapter will surprise and move you with its unique format and flow, while also inviting you to find forgiveness and build resilience.

A few short days after meeting **Monika Nielsen** for the first time at a networking meeting, we scheduled a playdate with our kids at the park so we could talk about the vision for this book. We resonated with each other so deeply that it didn't take much for her to come aboard. Monika is one of those people who just makes you feel at home—no judgements. And that's why her chapter fits beautifully with the theme of forgiving yourself. In her business, she opens up a safe space for women to be vulnerable, and that's exactly what she's done in these pages.

Vesta Hager and I met through a networking group, but truly, it feels like we've known each other for a lifetime. We are so alike, and I couldn't imagine an Empowered Woman collaboration book without her. Vesta's can-do attitude about everything in life is what entrepreneurship is all about—and also why we're so similar. It is our goal to help women see there's nothing standing in their way except their self-imposed limitations. And that's where forgiveness comes in: it's okay to realize we've been stopping ourselves from pursuing our dreams. Now is the time to take the center stage of our lives and shine!

THE POWER IN U

By Barbara Conway

HE OVERSIZED LEATHER rocking chair enveloped me in its comforting embrace as I reclined, almost sideways, covered in a fluffy gray blanket. My gaze fell upon the array of pill bottles neatly lined up on the coffee table. "It would be so easy," I whispered to myself, contemplating the idea of taking them all and succumbing to a deep slumber. It was Monday morning, my day off. My kids had gone back to their dad's house, our family home, for the week—leaving me alone in a mobile home where we had practically started our family. This was my space now, or it would be, eventually, after the divorce was final.

Memories of the happy, loving family I had once created in this house flooded my mind, but as I opened my eyes, I was confronted with empty rooms and minimal hand-me-down furniture from my departed loved ones. I wondered which of my kids would appreciate the comfort of this big, cozy chair. Just as I reached down to grab the first bottle, Lil Bit, my Pomeranian, hopped onto my lap, reminding me that I was not alone. Meanwhile, CJ, my Standard Poodle, nudged me, reminding me to take him outside. It was like he knew what I was thinking and wanted to redirect me by reminding me he was there. Smiling at that sweet face that loved me unconditionally and depended on me for so much, I set the pill bottle aside and headed to retrieve their leashes.

This was the daily/hourly battle I faced when my children left for the week to go to their dad's. My high school sweetheart and husband of 25 years wanted another. I had invested 34 years of my life and secured a future for our family after his retirement from the military—and it was all gone. Four words destroyed my dream life: "I want a divorce". I had very little formal education, and I have always done what I needed to do to support him in his military career and in helping run our sign company. My job working with the military placed me in the uncomfortable situation of continuing to work with his best friends and "Battle Buddies". I just knew they were talking about me. They all pretty much quit speaking to me. I began to see that my life, marriage, and career were all finished.

The rocking chair became my sanctuary, offering solace in the quiet, lonely times. Why did I resist those pills? The dogs, needing their walks, provided a lifeline whenever I was tempted by medicine bottles. CJ and my trio of Pomeranians stood guard, deterring me each time I contemplated the unthinkable. They craved cuddles, their meals were a must, and they insisted on outdoor excursions. Although CJ was too large to climb up in my chair, we often found comfort on the floor, where my tears flowed freely, particularly around bedtime.

The mantle of motherhood had abruptly vanished, leaving a huge void. The purpose that had driven me for the past 19 years was now stripped away every alternate week. No more reminders for baths, ensuring teeth were brushed, or bedtime routines. The emptiness was consuming as this depression held on tight to me. Having cooked for a family of five or more, it was hard to cook for one. So, I didn't, and my appetite waned. This was my reality for months on end. Eventually, I glimpsed my reflection at a mere 90 pounds, a stark 30-pound weight loss evident. Frailty stared back, and an emptiness resided within me.

And yet, here I am. Today, I am the proud mother of three amazing kids, who are now grown. At the time of this writing, my youngest is about to graduate high school. Although CJ and Bella have now passed, I still have Bit and Moo. I recently added two Chiweenies to my household—Isabelle, Izzy for short, and Ginger. I fully credit my dogs for saving my life in 2015. CJ was the best friend I could've had while going through all of that.

I also recognize the training I have received in my, now, 33 years of working with the Louisiana National Guard. As a volunteer, I learned valuable communication skills, problem-solving techniques, and how to deal with personality differences. In 2003, I was hired as a family assistance coordinator and have learned more about resiliency, suicide prevention, and financial literacy. When I saw myself in the mirror that day, I drew on all that information, and over the next few months, pulled myself out of depression. I also found *power* in red lipstick—more on that later.

As I was getting dressed for work one morning, I realized I could finally pursue my passions without any constraints, allowing me to delve into subjects that truly interested me. This newfound freedom empowered me to shape my educational journey according to my own aspirations. My future was wide open. I didn't have to ask for permission to do anything. I could join a MLM or start my own business.

While working from home in 2020, I found the online world of life coaching. I had mentored soldiers, airmen, and their families for years, and I absolutely loved what I did. I realized I could use my well-honed skills to help other women who were suffering as I was— women who suddenly found themselves lost, trying to find their own identity, or just attempting to overcome a challenge. I dove, headfirst, into more personalized professional development and completed two yearlong courses. I emerged as a certified mindset coach with an understanding of the power of manifestation and positive thinking.

I was on the struggle bus for a few years, trying to find a professional path outside of work that aligned with my values. The only thing I had created in my first five years was my veteran nonprofit, a networking group of veteran service organizations that works together as a team to close the gaps in services for our local veterans. Throughout this eight-year journey, I can recognize three significant breakthroughs that helped me. These breakthroughs gave me purpose to A.C.T.

ACCOUNTABILITY:

This was an issue for me. I recognized I had a problem with suicidal ideations, low self-esteem, and my confidence was shot. I made some poor choices. I spent money where I shouldn't have and followed the gurus of social media, but I really focused on my life in 2020. This was a time of self-reflection as we all navigated life during lockdown. I realized I had to have an accountability partner. Of the amazing women I spoke to as I began to create my life as it is now, I found two perfect mentors/coaches. In the past years, I have had the pleasure of learning from others, as well. I gained the clarity I needed to move forward, organizational skills to balance work, business, and kids every other week, and discovered what exactly I wanted for my life.

Are you in a place where you find yourself wondering "Is There Life Out There", as Reba sang? Are you asking what to do with yourself now that the kids have moved out, you've had a career change or retirement, gotten divorced, been widowed, or just plain started questioning your life? Maybe you're frustrated, thinking you were meant to do great things, and are at a loss as to what that looks like. Having the accountability from a supportive person who understood the vision I wanted for my future was invaluable. Being able to craft a tangible action plan from a mentor that actually cared if I succeeded was exactly what I needed to get to where I am today.

COMMITMENT:

While my past demons had a tight hold on my subconscious, I had to continuously battle with them to remember everything I had accomplished. I had 30+ years of experience serving the Louisiana National Guard and their families throughout the state, 20 years as an entrepreneur who had built our sign company to over $100,000 in worth in less than two years, and a 25-year track record of being a loving, supportive, and loyal military spouse. I had also overcome the most traumatic event in my life, alone. I had to believe I could do anything I set my mind to. I was the product of the Army as a military spouse with countless deployments and state emergency activations, such as flooding or tornadoes, under her belt. While I had always been committed to someone else, I had to learn to be committed to myself and my goals. I soon learned that I wasn't starting over—I was beginning again with new knowledge. #gamechanger

I was terrified to step outside my comfort zone! I felt guilty for putting myself first, but it was my turn to commit to myself and create the future I wanted. It was not easy. Realization is only the first step. Having that mentor to remind me to stay true to my vision, to do the work it took to get where I am today, was key. I decided I was going to do it. Failure was not an option.

THANKFULNESS:

Gratitude has been such a vital part of my growth these past few years. I have learned to sit, be still, and reflect on my life. I accept my past and am thankful for the lessons I have learned. While I am not pleased with how things transpired, I am thankful that the woman in my ex-husband's life loves my children as her own. I am eternally grateful that their precious seven-year-old half-sister brings such joy to them—and me, as well. I am also thankful for the people God placed in my life over the years, including my work family.

Remember that red lipstick I mentioned earlier? My supervisor insisted I get and wear red lipstick. Little did

I know that she was making me do my self-care. Every woman knows you just can't wear red lipstick—the process of putting on your makeup just so you can wear that red lipstick is empowering in itself. This was such a revelation to me and sparked a whole new attitude.

Fast forward to the summer of 2022, and she asked if I had started my own lipstick line when I asked if I could show her one of my personal accomplishments. If you read chapter four of *Think and Grow Rich*, you will learn not to let any idea slip past. Once I committed to this, things fell into place, and by October, I had launched Empowered by BTC—my very own lip gloss line with colors named after women that have inspired me in my life. This makes three businesses and a nonprofit I have created—all while working full time! I am so grateful for the things I have accomplished in the past few years. I never would've done them had I been married.

You can do this, too. When you are in the right frame of mind and listen to what God, or the Universe, is telling you, you are motivated to ACT.

In conclusion, I hope your biggest take away from this chapter is to never give up. My Army training is a valuable asset, but one I neglected while I was in the throes of that debilitating depression. I had to go through the worst part of my life to realize I am special and worthy of a happy life. I swallowed my pride and asked for help. My mentors came to me at the right time, and I got the personalized help I needed—help that allowed me to move past my trauma and change my focus to the future. I began my life again with the vision of a single empty nester, with four dogs.

The women in my life have educated me on what is possible when you believe in yourself, and they have my undying gratitude. My passion is to help others, and my years working with the military have taught me valuable lessons. I truly love what I do and live for my days in the office or helping around the state. The purpose of my veteran nonprofit, Military Assistance Community Resource Alliance (MACRA) is to fill the gaps in service in my community as well as across the state. There are a lot of resources out there for active duty, but not many for Guardsmen and Reservists. The mission of MACRA is to advocate for these service men and women while filling these gaps in veteran care.

The lip gloss line, EmpoweredbyBTC.com, speaks for itself. As I begin to create names for the next group of colors, I plan to make this interactive. Soon, anyone will be able to submit nominations for the next set of colors. My life as a travel advisor has also been rewarding. I have booked cruises for years but am just now getting into booking all-inclusive resorts. Finally, I have just launched a membership for encouragement and self-development. There are five areas of personal development that I felt were vital in my transformation. These areas are: Confidence, Goal Setting, Mindset, Procrastination, and Purpose. I invite you to join us at NextUbyBTC.com and on my blog at BarbaraConway.com.

Life is truly what you make of it. My dogs saved my life for a reason. My coworkers and those soldiers I serve are now *my* "Battle Buddies", but more importantly, they are my family. I know I have a higher purpose. I am here to help others manage the rough spots in life. My clients come to me for many different reasons—personal or business, I am able to talk them through most any challenge. Being a 4/6 Projector in Human Design, I feel that I am truly living my purpose.

As I begin my life as an empty nester, I am proud of the fact that I have raised children who love and depend on one another. I feel excited for my future and continued plans to develop the life I dream about. My next chapter is just beginning. This time, I walk into it with confidence and the passion to serve others in their need to create the life of their dreams.

FOUR STEPS TO UNLEASH YOUR INNERBLISS GODDESS

By Bella Bliss

*G*ROWING UP IN a utopian middle-class, suburbia, stable environment, I never thought I would end up in a toxic relationship with a narcissist. This relationship left me feeling lost, confused, disoriented, and disconnected. I told myself, "I didn't grow up like this—I don't know how I ended up here!"

For two decades, I remained silent about the abuse I experienced in a toxic and controlling marriage. I was lost and felt so far away from my true self, but on the Lion's Gate portal in 2015, I set the intention to no longer be a victim of circumstance and to live according to my own choice. This was the beginning of my quest to find my soul's purpose and my own, unique path.

The Lion's Gate portal is a powerful tool for unlocking our intentions and amplifying our spiritual energy. I used this energy to immerse myself into a shamanic journey and saw myself as a male lion. I knew my spirit animal was the lion, but seeing this strong, proud male lion was the beginning of a rebirth of my new identity—and many deaths of the old me.

This was truly transformative, and my shift in consciousness was such a revelation, as I had never seen myself as a leader or protector in the physical sense. In the spiritual sense, I had always known I was different, but that day, my power was unleashed.

Using daily practices and the power of love from that day forward, I shed my old self and embraced my inner truth through the powerful force of my lion essence. I began to face fear with courage and use it as fuel to light my path. I realized that we are not meant to live in survival mode, but to trust ourselves and make empowered choices. Like the lion, we rest and spring into action only when necessary. This realization was a way of transmuting my beliefs from powerlessness to power.

Power can be seen in different ways. I hadn't seen myself as a warrior in the sense of fighting and forcing, nor did I power my way through life. But with the power of love and light, I learned that we could become warriors of the light and do this with the intention of leading the way for others to find their own fire that burns from within. And this is what I set out to do—to find my way through my own spiritual path to greatness so that I can become the powerful person I was truly meant to be.

The Lion's Gate portal was a life-changing moment for me, and it can be for anyone who decides to face the darkness with courage and embrace their inner power. With the power of intention and the Lion's Gate portal, when I set out to do things according to my choice, I was no longer a victim of circumstance.

By embracing my newfound truth and surrendering to the wave of my own soul-fire, I began to live with Spirit. This journey of love, courage, and inner knowing allowed me to develop strength and clarity, enabling me to see life in a new light—my own. By doing this, I realized I was already the person I knew I was meant to be. I became limitless.

In our human conditioning, we are born *imprisoned* by a broken system. Navigating our own spiritual path requires us to embrace empowerment and let go of fear because when we are living our life in a world of fear, our instinct is to contract, be silent, and remain small to avoid standing out. We live in constant defense, unable to truly experience life.

I learned through breathwork, yoga, and meditation that we have an inner strength that can illuminate our path forward, so that we can have the type of life we want to remember. These modalities regulate the nervous system and help the body to embrace rest, so we can spring into action when necessary—just like the lion.

Through a deeper connection to my true self, I learned to live with universal power.

Living with Spirit, becoming limitless, and living in universal power are the ways I began living my true, authentic life by following my heart, giving myself grace, and trusting my inner guidance system, which I call my InnerBLISS GPS. We all have this divine guidance available to us from within. We just need to pay attention to our intentions and lead with our own light so we can navigate our way through any storm. Basically, we become our own lighthouse in the great sea of life.

Through this chapter, I want to help you become your own lighthouse.

For me, this process began with making agreements with myself:

1. I chose to stop being harsh and began practicing self-compassion.

When I felt uncomfortable, I reminded myself that it was okay. I stopped judging, blaming, shaming, and guilting myself and others. When negative thoughts arose, I reframed them and focused on gratitude. This powerful practice allowed me to start laughing and loving life and remembering what it was like to be innocent and play. I began to play in my own quantum playground of limitless possibilities and became the creator of my reality.

2. I began trusting and respecting myself.

I moved forward and embraced the realization that *I* was the shift. Everything began to revolve around my frequency of being. This revelation changed my world, and I share it with you because it's easy to get caught up in trying to control life, which makes us lose sight of our true identity.

3. I committed to surrendering to the flow of life, and by doing this, I shifted into a higher frequency.

This required becoming aware of my old patterns and energy and learning to master the art of being myself.

Alignment of the body, mind, and spirit fuels the flame of our full potential so we can unleash it and live life to the fullest. However, it's not uncommon for people to feel stuck because of the hold of their old patterns, and sometimes, they even feel like they have failed when they can't change them. It's important to know that there is a solution to these disempowering thoughts and emotions.

Most of the time, we wake up in a world that doesn't align with our expectations, and our unconscious mind kicks in on autopilot. Once we awaken to our reality, we may feel disappointed, lacking, or defeated. But with the right strategies and mindset, we can overcome these feelings.

Sometimes, we may resort to old patterns of self-defeating and self-sabotaging behavior, leading us back to the same disempowering situations. This is where many people may feel lost and broken. You are not alone!

Feeling overwhelmed and stuck in life is a common experience, especially as we age and lose sight of our goals. It's easy to get lost in the maze of our mind and the default behaviors it leads us to, but there is a way out.

This leads me to my next point, which is that you must cultivate a positive relationship with yourself and focus your energy inward, so you can uncover your unique talents and learn to embrace your inner power.

o.I began a spiritual journey of self-discovery.

By learning to be conscious of your unconscious mind, you will learn to become your own victor, rather than being a victim. I started by asking myself better questions to gain deeper insights into my true nature, versus the reactions that were rooted in the way I'd always been and done things. I also invested in a mastery course of communication and connection via personality typing tools such as the Enneagram, followed by delving into

Human Design. I learned so much about the human psyche and where we are in healthy expression and what happens when we are unhealthy and misaligned with our true nature.

I find it absolutely fascinating how unique we are and how we all perceive the world differently, both in our light and in our shadow selves. I believe that our individuality is so profound that there is no point in comparing ourselves to others. Something magical happens when you start radiating energy inwards and focus on your own soul-fire.

With these four steps in momentum, I came to another crossroad with my new identity of courage and survival. Now what? I learned how to become a thriver! I remembered what it was like to live again! I continued upleveling in my own way, on my own terms, and discovered how to embrace my true powers, gifts, and talents and began exploring them. I continued following my InnerBLISS GPS by expanding my conscious mind to allow my creative powers to guide my way and ditched the old, unconscious autopilot that was keeping me stuck and lost.

This is what led me to igniting the way for my InnerBLISS Goddess to be fully unleashed! All my experiences and challenges helped me face the fire and go through it. I became the fire, dancing in it and around it, formless and limitless.

One day, I said to myself that I had spiritual gifts and needed to explore them. I started working with a spiritual coach, and that is what happened.

I leaned into full trust and intuition, which guided me into a meditation where I saw her—she was powerfully ablaze as the Fire Dragon Goddess. In her red cape, her magnetizing and mysterious divine essence, I saw her. She was there all along. I was so connected to her that I felt that I was her.

And then I realized... I am her!

You know all those divine breadcrumbs and nudges you get? All those things that you feel stirring inside of you, but you are too afraid to share them with anyone because you may sound crazy? All those red flags that you later say you should have followed because they were a warning to do or not to do something, but you went against them anyway? All those divine synchronicities that you experience?

Yes, that is her. She is within all of us. She is waiting to be unleashed. All those fiery emotions, those exciting, adventurous things that you want to do or be part of. All those wild ideas, deep inner wisdom, and divine "downloads" that are unexpressed. Yes, they are her, too!

We go through life stuffing her down, shutting her out, holding her back and suppressing her. We do the very thing that we, as women, despise.

Do you feel her? Do you want to feel courageous, too? To stand in your power and speak your truth? Do you want to feel empowered and in your joy—always? Do you want to start living the life that you are excited to live and begin living your legacy now?

Do you want to be fully expressed, courageous, complete, whole, satisfied, aligned, grounded, balanced, centered, confident, clear, and successful in everything you do? Do you want to feel like you are doing everything wholeheartedly and giving from an overflow and playing full out in your own playground of limitless possibilities?

You can! You can do it all! You are limitless.

However, ask yourself, what would it feel like to truly live like that? What would that look like? How would you imagine yourself to be this way? What are you wearing in that scenario? How does it feel to be her? Can you connect with her? Have you connected with her before? Does she love to dance, does she love to create, does she love to lead with freedom in her bright light and vivid vision of divine peace, unconditional love, laughter, joy, and bliss every day?

What types of qualities does she have? What would it feel like to embrace everything about her and integrate her into your life? What would it feel like to *be* her?

I encourage you to explore your InnerBLISS Goddess and unleash her! Embody her amazing superpowers and ignite all the sparks within you to connect with her and become her. Stoke the flames every day so you become a trailblazer to lead the path for others, like me. And if you need to use the powers of my Fire Dragon Goddess for inspiration, I invite you to!

Allow my InnerBLISS Fire Dragon Goddess power, courage, passion, strength, creativity, and wisdom to inspire and empower you!

In fact, by harnessing the harmony of the divine feminine with the divine masculine, we can live in duality with the ease, grace, and the flow of life by surrendering to it by letting go of trying to control it, force it, or fight it.

Joy is our birthright, and we create our quantum reality of infinite possibilities. We are the ocean that is the collective waves of consciousness. We are the energy that moves to us and through us. We become the solution and experiences we seek when we become the empowered InnerBLISS Goddess.

We live our legacy by embracing mystery and truly living the life we want to remember, unapologetically. You are already part of the oneness, the wholeness, the completeness of universal power and the divinity that is within. All you need to do is unleash her!

The soul only knows love.

In this truth, I now guide my clients through their own journeys, helping them to live with their own universal power, with Spirit, and limitlessly, as if they already have what their soul-fire desires. They learn to lead with vision and lean into their own inner knowing, inner wisdom, and InnerBLISS happiness.

This profound experience enables them to venture into the unknown, embrace the mystery of life with courage, and ultimately, bridge the gap so that they can live a life beyond what they ever thought possible. This is how our divine breadcrumbs lead us to the quantum surprises that we create, just by "being". In our conditioning, we are so invested into the "doing" of life that we forget or never really know how to simply live *in* our life.

I invite you to read my bio at the end of this book to learn how to connect with me and gain access to free resources. Let me walk you through the path of finding your InnerBLISS GPS, your inner Goddess, your fire within.

Your authentic you is waiting to be unveiled. If not now, then when?

WINGS OF BRILLIANCE

By Paris Byrum

In the depths of despair, a broken bird I stood,
With tattered wings and wounds so deep, misunderstood.
A captive in a cage of fear and sorrow's sway,
But hope's flickering ember refused to fade away.

My spirit, once vibrant, now worn and frail,
Engulfed by shadows, lost within a tempest's gale.
Yet a glimmer of light pierced through the darkest night,
A Hand reached out, whispered, "Rise, take flight."

With trembling heart, I dared to spread my wings,
To soar beyond the pain, where freedom sweetly sings.
Embracing Grace's breeze, I shed the chains that bind,
And discovered strength in the recesses of my mind.

Through the valleys of despair, I stumbled and fell,
In the depths of brokenness, my spirit started to swell.
Like a phoenix rising from the ashes, renewed,
I found the power in Christ, my purpose imbued.

The scars that marked my past, now tales to share,
For in their etchings, resilience and triumph flare.
With every flap, a symphony of healing resounds,
As I dance with the winds, on redemption's hallowed grounds.

No longer a captive, no longer bound,
I spread my wings wide, a melody profound.
In the vast expanse, I find solace, I find peace,
As my brokenness transforms, Grace's sweet release.

A chorus of voices echoes through the sky,
Carrying the tale of a broken bird, learning how to fly.
With each beat of my heart, a resounding refrain,
A testament to the brilliance of a soul unchained.

So, dear reader, take heed of this soaring flight,
Unleash the shackles that hinder your own light.
Embrace the power of Christ, let your brilliance shine,
For you, too, can ascend, in a journey so Divine.

In the symphony of life, let your voice be heard,
As evidenced by the broken bird's triumphant word.
Through struggles faced, redemption's song unfurls,
And in the end, you'll rise, healed, to new heights, a new
world.

THE BROKEN BIRD

In the depths of despair, I found myself trapped within
the suffocating confines of an abusive marriage. For years,
I endured the relentless storm of emotional and physical
torment that battered my spirit. Anxiety and depression
became unwelcome companions, weaving their tendrils
through every facet of my being as the weight of the abuse
grew heavier with each passing day.

Like a fragile bird with broken wings, I was stripped of my confidence and left adrift in a sea of despair. The walls of my own mind held me captive, echoing with the venomous words and cruel actions inflicted upon me. I longed for freedom, but fear and doubt shackled me, chaining me to a life I believed I could never escape.

Picture a lone tree, battered by fierce winds and torrential rain. Its branches strain against the tempest, threatening to snap under the weight of the storm. But deep within its core, a spark of resilience flickers—a quiet reminder of its innate strength. Just as that tree finds the will to stand tall against the elements, so, too, did I discover an inner fortitude—a glimmer of hope that refused to be extinguished.

Join me on this journey as I navigate the treacherous waters of abuse and emerge transformed. Amidst the trials and tribulations that lie ahead, the challenges that threaten to consume me, I will discover the power to homeschool my six precious children, minister to other women trapped in darkness, and lead a life brimming with productivity and purpose. This is the story of my redemption—a testament to the transformative power of faith.

LIFE IN THE DARKNESS

In the suffocating grip of my abusive marriage, every day seemed like a descent further into darkness. Spiritual oppression permeated the air, as my ex-husband twisted the sacred teachings of the Bible to manipulate and control me. Verbal lashings became routine, tearing away at my self-worth, while outbursts of rage echoed through the home, leaving me trembling in fear. The violence escalated, with fists pounding into walls, leaving behind shattered plaster and punctured dreams. The children and I lived in constant fear, our hearts in trepidation with each unpredictable step, always on edge, never knowing when the next explosion would occur.

The toll on my mental and emotional well-being was immeasurable. Anxiety wrapped its icy fingers around my chest, squeezing tighter with each passing day. Depression clouded my thoughts, casting a shadow over even the simplest of joys. My spirit felt crushed under the weight of constant criticism and the relentless onslaught of emotional abuse. I became a shell of the woman I once was, my identity eclipsed by the fear and despair that engulfed me.

Coping became an insurmountable challenge. There were days when I couldn't bear to get out of bed, weighed down by the heaviness in my soul. The immense pressure forced me to make a heart-wrenching decision—I had to send my children to school after five years of homeschooling. It felt like another loss, another piece of myself being sacrificed to the constant demands of an unbearable situation. The guilt gnawed at me, as I questioned my worth as a mother and mourned the loss of the nurturing environment I had fought so hard to create.

In the darkness of that marriage, I was trapped, my spirit broken, and my hope smoldering like a dying flame. Little did I know that glimmers of light would soon begin to seep through the cracks, leading me toward a path of liberation and transformation.

FINDING HOPE IN FAITH

In the midst of my darkest days, a ray of light pierced through the glowering clouds of dejection in the form of a compassionate companion. This person, overflowing with empathy, walked alongside me, offering solace and understanding. With gentle words and unwavering support, they helped me see the profound impact of the oppression I had endured. Through their presence, I began to realize that I was not alone in my suffering.

It was within this journey of pain and awakening that I discovered the transformative power of Christ. In the depths of my anguish, I turned to God, seeking peace and answers. Through prayer and reflection, I witnessed the goodness and love that radiated from His divine presence. It was a revelation amidst the chaos and despair. However, I must admit that I, initially, resisted fully surrendering to God's healing touch. I clung to self-sufficiency, believing that I could mend my broken wings on my own. But I couldn't do it... I came to the end of myself. Yet, just as a bird with shattered wings needs a skilled healer to restore its ability to fly, I began to recognize the limitations of my own strength.

In moments of vulnerability, I allowed God to work within me, to mend the brokenness that had consumed my soul. I relinquished control and embraced the power of surrender, knowing that true transformation could only be achieved through divine intervention. With each step toward faith, I felt God's gentle touch, slowly and purposefully repairing the broken pieces of my being. And as my wings mended, I soared to new heights, guided by the love and grace of the One who had walked beside me all along.

STEWARDING MY BODY, TIME, AND MIND

With newfound strength and determination, I embarked on a journey of self-care and prioritizing my physical health. Recognizing the toll the oppressive marriage had taken on my body, I began to invest in activities that nurtured and restored it. From daily exercise routines to nutritious meals, I consciously chose to treat my body as a temple, honoring the vessel that housed God's Spirit.

Reclaiming my time became a crucial step in my path to freedom. I realized the importance of establishing boundaries, both with my ex-spouse and with others who might use God's word to further entrap my mind. With resolute resolve, I learned to say "no" to obligations that did not align with my God-given purpose and "yes" to activities that spurred on my faith. It was a process of self-discovery, as I carved out moments for self-reflection, creativity, and prayer.

As I delved deeper into my faith, I recognized the power of renewing my mind through studying and applying God's word. I immersed myself in the teachings of Christ, finding solace and guidance within the sacred scriptures. I sought wisdom from trusted mentors and engaged in meaningful discussions with fellow believers. Each revelation became a steppingstone, reshaping my perspective and empowering me to overcome the lingering effects of the abuse. Through prayer, meditation, and the daily application of biblical principles, I forged a renewed mindset that was anchored in love, grace, and perseverance. Poems and song lyrics were often my encouragement through these tough times. Hope is something that must be clung to, just like this poem describes:

"Hope" is the thing with feathers[7]
By Emily Dickinson

"Hope" is the thing with feathers -
That perches in the soul -
And sings the tune without the words -
And never stops–at all -
And sweetest–in the Gale–is heard -
And sore must be the storm -
That could abash the little Bird
That kept so many warm -
I've heard it in the chillest land -
And on the strangest Sea -
Yet–never–in Extremity,
It asked a crumb–of me.

FLYING FREE

The realization that I needed to leave the oppressive marriage dawned upon me, illuminating a path toward liberation. However, this decision was not without its challenges. Within the Christian community, the belief in the permanence of marriage was deeply entrenched, and some viewed divorce as absolutely unacceptable. Wrestling with the fear of judgment and the weight of societal expectations, I found myself caught between the desire for deliverance and the fear of disappointing others.

[7] Dickinson, Emily. ""Hope" Is the Thing with Feathers." Poetry Foundation. Accessed September 12, 2023. https://www.poetry-foundation.org/poems/42889/hope-is-the-thing-with-feathers-314.

The fear of man, intertwined with the fear of God's judgment, threatened to paralyze me. It was a daunting journey to navigate, as I confronted the clash between my own well-being and the expectations of my faith community. However, as I sought counsel from wise and discerning individuals and churches, I discovered a nuanced understanding of biblical divorces and the compassionate nature of God's love. They understood that divorce, in certain circumstances, can be a means of restoration and protection, and I found refuge in the loving embrace of those who saw beyond the surface and recognized the complexities of my situation. Their steady support and guidance provided me with the courage to embrace my decision and break free from the chains of this marriage, enabling me to rise above the fear of man.

THE FINAL FLIGHT

In the next chapter of my journey, I would discover the strength and brilliance within myself, because of Christ, as I stepped into a life filled with possibilities, empowered by my faith, and surrounded by a community that championed my freedom and healing.

In the depths of despair, I discovered the power of faith, the resilience of the human will, shaped by God's word, and the transformative love of Jesus Christ. My journey from the darkness of an abusive marriage to a life of hope and purpose was not without its challenges, but it has left me with a profound sense of empowerment, hope, and inspiration. As I reflect upon my story, I invite you to embark on your own journey of brilliance in Christ, where productivity and fulfillment can be found amidst life's trials.

1. Embrace your faith: Cultivate a deep relationship with God, for in Him lies the source of strength, wisdom, and guidance. Seek His presence through prayer, study His Word, and engage with a community of believers who can support and encourage you along the way.

2. Nurture self-care: Prioritize your physical, mental, and emotional well-being. Steward your body by adopting healthy habits, exercise, and proper nutrition. Take time for self-reflection, pursue hobbies and interests that bring you joy, and seek professional help when needed.

3. Establish boundaries: Learn to say no to obligations and commitments that do not align with your values or drain your energy. Set healthy boundaries with unhealthy relationships and situations that hinder your growth and well-being. Create a space for yourself where you can thrive and flourish.

4. Seek personal growth: Continuously pursue personal and professional goals that align with Christ's virtues and your passions. Invest in education, skill development, and press into sanctification. Surround yourself with mentors and like-minded individuals who can inspire and challenge you to reach your fullest potential.

5. Serve and inspire others: As you navigate your own journey, extend a helping hand to others

who may be facing similar challenges. Share your story, offer support and encouragement, and be a source of hope for those who are hurting. By ministering to others, you will not only make a positive impact on their lives but also experience the fulfillment that comes from being a vessel of God's love and compassion.

Throughout my journey, God has held me in His gentle hand, unwavering even when my faith was wavering. In the face of adversity, He was my anchor, grounding me amidst the storms of life. His word provided me with the strength to persevere when the road seemed unbearable and reminded me of the eternal hope that awaited me. Like a bird with mended wings, I soared to new heights, redeemed and healed by Jesus.

As I steward this life of brilliance that God has made in me, I strive to maintain a delicate balance. I am reminded that brilliance does not mean perfection, but rather embracing the unique gifts and talents bestowed upon us by our Creator. It is a continual process of surrender and alignment with God's purpose for our lives. By relying on His guidance and wisdom, we can lead lives that are not only productive, but also filled with purpose and significance.

May my story be a testament to the power of Christ, the tenacity of the human will, and the transformative love of God. May it inspire you to embark on your own journey of brilliance, where you find hope, empowerment, and contentment. May you spread your wings and soar to new heights, guided by faith and embraced by the all-encompassing love of our Heavenly Father.

WALK WITH ME IF YOU WILL

By Monika Nielsen

*W*E'RE HEADED TO your closet. Yes, I know that makes you feel slightly uncomfortable. I tell you that I've seen it all and that there's no judgment, and you send up a silent prayer that I'm telling you the truth. Thinking quickly and wondering what's on the floor that you may have missed, you're feeling embarrassed that it's not Pinterest perfect. It may be a bit cluttered, but it's really the annoyance of getting ready in the morning and the discontent you feel with the few choices in your wardrobe that has led you to me. You're tired of flipping aggressively through your hangers, furiously digging through your drawers, with the anxiety of "What do I wear today?" looming as you need to get yourself together.

So, we keep walking.

As we get closer, your chest gets a little tighter, and you talk a little faster. You tell me all about the pieces you are waiting to get back into when you achieve some future goal or another.

"Those extra pounds just don't come off like they used to," you sigh, hoping I'll understand.

You know that when we walk in, we'll see the graveyard of clothes that could have been... the things you wore when life was different, the pieces that still have tags on them because you couldn't pass up a "great deal".

"It would be so wasteful to just throw them away," you repeat to yourself, again and again.

So, here we are.

We are standing in your closet, but you feel we are looking at your life! Because that's the thing about closets—they hold the items that we hold closest to ourselves each and every day, and so we aren't just looking at your clothes. We are looking at how you have lived in the past and how you are showing up right now.

You feel a bit awkward and self-conscious. Your cheeks are getting a little warm, and your heart's beating a little more rapidly.

I want to hug you and tell you that it's going to be okay. You're not alone, not the only one that feels like this. I understand because I've been there and know exactly how you feel.

LET'S TAKE A LOOK BACK

Let me tell you about my own closet crisis in 2017.

I was standing, naked, in my closet, as we do, desperately trying to find something that fit my body *and* made me feel beautiful. My only pair of jeans had just become so worn they broke through right in the spot the thighs rub together—couldn't even be fixed.

"Great," came the exasperated sigh, when obviously I felt anything but great. Now what? A new pair? But I had told myself I wouldn't buy anything until I lost those 20 lbs. And so began the internal struggle. Why did I care so much about size? I was a grown woman—what was I doing? Shouldn't I have known better than to let this pair of jeans determine my self-worth? Good God, it was just a piece of cloth!

When I look back now at how much I tied my self-esteem to a certain size or a certain brand, it's embarrassing. I thought I had evolved past that—and I had! I had done the work and understood my triggers but was slowly going off course over several years. By the time my crisis closet came around, I was determined by sheer will that I was going to fit back into those jeans. You know why?

Because it was *something I had always been able to control.*

And at that time in my life, most things felt totally out of control. There was the strain and trauma of a very complicated pregnancy and (almost) year of recovery that followed. Then, I lost my mother a year later. Oh, hello grief, what do I do with you? I didn't have time to grieve—I had a newborn and two other children to homeschool with a husband that traveled all the time.

And then there was the burden of figuring out health issues... one after another after another... with exhausting effort. I went through months of exhaustion while, simultaneously, not sleeping at night. I wondered if I was facing adrenal fatigue. Surely, a slow and steady extra 50 lbs crept on when I ate so healthy. Were my hormones jacked-up? Was it early menopause? Answers evaded me—and the doctor after doctor I sought out to help.

And because I couldn't control any of it, the idea of starving myself to get into those jeans felt like something appealing because it was all up to me.

Overlay this obsessive need to manage every detail with generational imprinting of "wastefulness", and it was a perfect storm. My grandmother was raised on a farm during the Depression and didn't have any luxuries and certainly never threw anything away. My mother was raised in that mentality, with a very low income, passing along the familial frugal philosophies.

And now me—a third generation of get-your-money's-worth-out-of-everything stood there, holding on to 90% of the beautiful closet I couldn't wear. I was determined to get back into it!

So, as I stared at my clothes, naked, with tears running down my face, I had one thought and one thought alone. *What is happening? This is insane!* The epiphany came to me out of nowhere. I realized that I was spiraling because of a piece of cloth and questioning my worth over articles of clothing I was keeping only out of guilt. Honestly, I couldn't believe how ridiculous it all was.

And so, I drew a line in the sand. I was not going to squeeze into a pair of jeans to remind myself not to eat. I was not going to bow my shoulders so much that my neck and back hurt because my chest had grown several sizes and I was trying to hide it. I was not going to keep torturing myself with ill-fitting clothing because it was wasteful to spend when I had so much. I would get ready every morning, looking at a closet full of beautiful clothing, mocking me with "motivation" until I achieved this goal of some arbitrary number I had in my head that was sure to make me happy. What a joke.

I was confused, annoyed, and a bit angry, but in that moment of clarity, here is what I knew to be true: If nothing changes, nothing changes.

Enough was enough. I was going to be worth getting dressed for the person I was *right then and there.* Screw the size. I needed these pieces of cloth to help me get dressed, not taunt me for not fitting into them. And that's exactly what I did.

So, when I say I can help you walk into a place of calm from the chaos of your closet and wardrobe, it's because I've made that journey and have helped hundreds of other women do the same. Our closets are our most vulnerable places. They carry all the blocked goals and unmet expectations of a life we don't have and a body we aren't particularly happy with.

But they also carry other feelings. The ones that are the most present are guilt, fear, and frustration.

LET'S WALK TOGETHER THROUGH SOME GUILT

The biggest shame is the money you feel you've wasted.

Think about it. Most of us don't think twice about spending more money on a good meal with friends. But honestly, what do you have to show for it besides memories? Did you beat yourself up over spending $14 on a lemon drop martini? Nope! Do you look at the jacket you spent too much money on now that you don't really wear it and feel guilty? Yep, kinda.

Why? Because it's staring at you every single time you step into your closet.

And then there's impulse shopping.

It looked *so good* on that Instagram model... but you got it, can't return it, and it didn't really fit your body or your life. So now you add another scornful reproach to yourself, "Why can't I just shop better?".

You're likely holding onto pieces from a life you no longer have. You've retired from your 9-5, yet those slacks still hang in your closet. Or, maybe, all the leggings you used to wear as a stay-at-home mom lie dormant while you now dress up for work each day. They're a reminder of what used to be, but you think it would be ridiculous to get rid of it all just because you're not wearing it. And psst, I'll tell you something that not a lot of people in my industry would say: You're right!

Take a good hard look at what you're not wearing.

If it is a maybe/perhaps, then keep it, but move it out of your space so you're not seeing it all the time. If you don't have another closet to store it, move it to the far left, far right, or in an under-the-bed box. You cannot continue to look at the things you aren't wearing and expect to feel good about where you are with your life or your size.

If it's a hard no, there are countless opportunities to give in your community. The very thing that sits in your closet, making you feel guilty every day, will be a huge blessing to others. You're not wearing it, and it could change the life of someone who needs it. Besides, it's a tax deduction. Everyone wins!

May I just ask that you give thoughtfully? Google local organizations to see where there's the highest need— smaller organizations make a much bigger impact than big-box donation centers. Start with Dress for Success or find an Assistance League in your town. There are often smaller thrift stores that will resell your items and use that money to fund other programs that do good in your community. What used to be your best things can become someone else's best things. Your current guilt over a jacket or pair of jeans can become a gift for someone else.

FEAR IS A CLOSE SECOND

Another strong emotion in our closet is fear, and it's a doozy. "If I give it away, will I have enough?" you anxiously wonder. "I may need that someday," you fret.

The dilemma here may be twofold.

Perhaps, in the past, you came from a place of need, so you feel a sense of security with lots of clothes in your closet. But please don't confuse security with choices and fulfillment.

Statistics show that we wear 23% of our wardrobe. If that is true for you, and you let go of the 73% that you never wear, you will be greeted every morning with all the things you wear right now! Everything you see, you can wear—that's true choice. Choice is *not* digging through the mess to find what you want, annoyance slowly building as you search for your favorite top.

Think about it. If it's not a piece you love, you're not getting dressed in anticipation of your day and how you need to show up in the world. You're getting dressed to put clothing on your body because you can't be naked at work.

Life is too short for that! Use these pieces of cloth to show the world who you are and what you can do! Get dressed and look in the mirror, beaming with a sense of feeling beautiful and secure in who you are.

But maybe you may have gone through this closet-edit thing already. You read a blog from a closet guru, grabbed your checklist, and spent the weekend going through, piece by piece, making decisions on your newfound guidelines.

You chucked it all, and it finally looks like those pretty Pinterest pictures of minimalist closets. You're waiting for the ease of getting dressed, the peace of a clean closet. But now you're bored. There is no joy in getting dressed, no "wow" pieces of color or patterns that make your eyes light up when you see yourself in the mirror.

The problem? You got rid of it all without knowing why!

With every client I work with, we dig into the *why* before the *how*. Why do you like what you like? Why don't you like what you don't? Why is your favorite sweater your favorite? Cut, fabric, style? It's the missing piece to purging intentionally.

I'm not a huge proponent of the popular minimalist philosophy of having 35-50 pieces of clothing for this perfect "Capsule Wardrobe". I love being creative with my clothing, and I feel I show up uniquely for the different areas of my life. If I want to be fun and flirty with my husband, I choose clothing that makes me feel fun and flirty! It will certainly be different than how I dress if I need to speak in front of a group. I'll wear a powerful color or cut of jacket at a presentation because it makes me feel self-assured. Chin up, shoulders back, great lipstick—let's go!

Now, let's get back in that closet and take a look with new guidelines. Don't throw it all away. Let us figure out your style, your life, and make sure your clothing reflects that.

If you're not wearing it due to size change or lifestyle change, take a hard, honest look at whether you should keep it or replace it with a piece more appropriate. If you're keeping it for that next goal, then get it out of your main closet space.

FRUSTRATION ROUNDS OUT THE THREE BIGGEST ISSUES IN OUR CLOSETS

Frustration... annoyance, irritation, discontent. They all mean the same thing. Frustration comes from a feeling of dissatisfaction, often accompanied by anxiety or depression, resulting from unfulfilled needs or unresolved problems.

You are playing a game of "Why can't I?" that is killing you! Why can't I... just stop shopping, just keep it clean, lose that weight.

Maybe it's a size thing, like mine was. You have all these things staring back at you, "motivating" you to be what was. And I hate to break it to you, but out of the hundreds of women I've helped, I've yet to see this work. Not only do you feel the silent judgment of those clothes that don't fit, but you also, almost always, blame yourself!

"Why can't I just stick to that diet?"

"Why did I go out with my friends last night to happy hour?"

"Why didn't I hit the gym this morning?"

Do you see what's happening? You are giving all this power to a piece of cloth. Your jeans don't know you're mad... but your family will pick up on it. Your friends will ask if you're okay. Because you spent the first 15 minutes of your day beating yourself up, it will affect your mood. That's a hard thing to come back from. And if you manage to let it go afterward, you've spent an enormous amount of energy talking yourself back into a good mental state. Countless studies tell us that clutter drains energy, consumes your precious time, reduces your working memory, and increases cognitive overload. Now you've double dipped with the negative self-talk. No wonder you're tired!

Enough! Would you talk to your best friend like that if she came to you for help? Would you berate your children for feeling distressed and overwhelmed?

Why are you starting out your day, already vulnerable, heaping on that kind of self-talk?

Clear out all the items that trigger those thoughts and feelings. If you are working on a goal, great! Move them to another closet. Box them up for your next phase. But, I cannot stress this enough, get them out of your visual space.

WALK WITH ME IF YOU WILL TO FREEDOM

There's a difference between holding onto a piece of clothing for the memories and holding onto a piece of clothing out of guilt.

There's a difference between shopping to fill the holes in your wardrobe and shopping to fill the holes in your life.

There's a difference between making good choices so that you can live a long, healthy life and starving yourself so that you can fit into an old pair of jeans.

I want you to know that it is possible to look in your closet, be delighted with your choices, and get ready quickly. Understanding the guilt, fear, and frustration that is hiding in your closet, alongside your clothing, is the first step to getting there.

It doesn't have to feel hard or overwhelming. You are worthy of feeling beautiful and having joy in getting ready.

CALLING ALL LEADING LADIES: IT'S YOUR TIME TO BE A STAR

By Vesta Hager

ARE YOU LIVING the life you want to live?

I'm willing to bet that you've never been asked this question and that no one in your circle of people would even want you to be asking it.

I doubt your children, your spouse, or your extended family really wants you living your dream. It isn't because they don't love you or want the best for you. I say this because, just like anyone else, they don't like change. And you living the life you want to live would probably be very impactful to them.

The people you love, support, cherish, and raise—they all have something they need from you. And that's a good thing, to have family and people that trust and rely on you.

But I'm here to ask: Isn't it time that you were living the life you want to lead?

Think about this question for a moment. What do you want your life to look like in this next chapter? What will bring you joy, energy, and passion? We can't afford to wait any longer for the "right" time to decide. The time is now.

I imagine that these thoughts have crossed your mind before, but we often don't put our feelings first when it comes to our family's needs. However, I know how it felt when things weren't right in my life. I realized that I felt like I was going through the motions and wasn't excited to get up in the morning and seize the day. I wondered where my passion had gone.

Have you felt this way, too?

You are not alone. We, women, tend to suffer in silence rather than believe we deserve something for ourselves. We tend to put our family's and friends' needs and activities before our own. We naturally think that there will be time for ourselves later.

But who defines when later has arrived? You do. Haven't you waited long enough?

As your children have grown, and you have had more time for yourself, you may have realized you don't know how to use it. I noticed that I filled it with other things to keep me busy. But being busy isn't my idea of a dream life—and it's probably not yours either.

If you are at this point in life, you may feel that you have waited too long or missed the chance to design your dream life. But there is still time. You just need to give yourself permission.

I predict that no one else will offer that—sometimes not even yourself. But it's time for you to design the life that you want to live. It is time because we, as women, can't wait another minute to be living that new life. It is time because our needs and desires matter just as much as everyone else's.

It is time because you deserve to feel like the star of your own movie. Step into the spotlight. We've been waiting for you.

So, I ask you again, are you living the life you want to live?

I hear your answer. No.

And that's okay, for now. For today. But it cannot be the final answer.

It is true, a great many women are stuck in that routine, and it's hard to break out of—and it's scary. Really scary. For you to make this change may seem daunting, but the real challenge is for those around you. Because I will state it right here.

Most of the people that you support, and love are not going to like that you're making these changes.

My revelation came in one of the many car lines I had sat in when my children were younger. Have you been in a car line? At soccer practices? Late night drama rehearsals? Spending your time waiting as they are following their passions?

I remember thinking about this as I sat there *two hours* before the bell. Waiting. I was early because if I wasn't the first car, I wasn't going to get out of there in time for their next event.

Our car line was epic. It wrapped around the neighborhood behind the school, twisting and turning and creating this slow, sad dirge to the pickup line. So, first I had to be, and my time was spent waiting.

I realized I was spending a lot of time in lines waiting for someone else's life to happen, waiting for them to have experiences and watching them grow. And that's a good thing. It's okay for them to have that and for you to be

THE EMPOWERED WOMAN'S PATH | 143

there for them. But it's also important that you have time for yourself. Then it hit me—I don't have any "me" time scheduled.

I knew that I had to make some changes. If I wanted a fulfilling and exciting life after raising those babies, it was up to me. I had to design my next life, my sequel. Having dreams or designing your life on a grand scale isn't something just for little kids or fairy tales. We all have the right to have purpose and to live our life the way we want to live it.

That day stuck with me because I knew that I needed to make changes. When the kids were young, I wanted to stay home with them. I made that choice, and I loved it. But as they got older, I realized that I wanted to think about what would come next. I knew I loved sharing and inspiring people with my words, my energy, my belief in their success. I had been a corporate trainer and a speaker—it was energizing, and I missed it.

I had skills. I just needed to dust them off. Maybe you need to do the same. I wanted to find what made me feel the joy I needed to feel, and that's what I want for you. I knew I was leading the way. I wanted to find a way to help other women through this transition. I knew if I could reach you, I could connect with you, and we could design our dream lives.

As I sat there in the pick-up line and had these revelations, it hit me that this was not going to be easy. But it was going to be worth it.

When you decide that you deserve the life you want to lead, and you decide that you're going to start making some changes to follow the dreams you have, there will be an impact on your life as it is.

There will be no status quo as you search and design your life. Things will be chaotic; family will push back when you aren't available all the time. They may say you are being selfish, that you don't have time for them anymore, that you are busy, and so on. But you will need to stay true to yourself.

I truly believe as we transition through this time, it will lead to something beautiful.

Most of the people I'm reaching out to right now have kids that are almost grown, almost out of the house, or at least out of school. Oftentimes, when the kids get older and, sometimes, leave, we find ourselves unprepared. Many women experience a great loss of identity and purpose. I want to mitigate or eliminate that time by *planning* for it. If you are in it, I have a plan for that, too. We will be sad that they are leaving, but that was our job—to raise them and release them. At our core, we are also proud of what they have accomplished and where they are going.

If they are moving out and on, it means we did our job. We sent them out to be young adults, contributing to society. You made that happen, so you should feel proud.

But the flipside is, if you don't prepare for an empty nest, you won't know who you are without them. But I'm telling you right now I know exactly who you are. You are a star.

You may have been recast in the last 18 years as a supporting role in your own movie. You may have moved out of the top cast to be listed just as nanny, unpaid Uber driver, laundress, cook, and personal shopper. You may have lost your own identity in the raising of others.

It is okay—you can recast yourself. It is *your* movie, after all.

You may have lost the part that you were literally born to play, but no worries. I am sharing a casting call right now, and you are perfect for the role.

OPEN CASTING CALL: *Please audition if you are a woman who put aside their dreams and desires and purpose to raise amazing human beings, care for loved ones, put someone else through school, or generally put your dreams on hold for anyone else.*

If you're not living the life you want, I am talking to you.

If your loss of identity is causing you to struggle every day, I am talking to you.

If you have depression over your loss of identity, I am talking to you.

If this transition has caused marital strife, I am talking to you.

If there are other issues that are cropping up that you never even thought of because you didn't have time in all those years of caring for these amazing people, yes, you guessed it—I am talking to you.

The first movie of your life ended with a bit of a cliffhanger. Your life as a mom was only your first role. *It is time to decide what you want your sequel to look like.*

Listen to me and repeat the next line:

I was born to play this role as the star in my own life movie.

Say it again. Write it on sticky notes and put it all over your house, your car, your bathroom mirror. You need to believe it as much as I already do. I know you are the STAR, and I am opening that casting call so I can tell you, so you can hear me. I already believe in the life you want to create, and I can help you create it.

You are not supporting cast material; you are the leading lady, and you need to step back into that role.

I have one question.

Is your dream worth it?

DREAM

Now, to pursue our dreams. We have secured the time, and when we get to this point in our life, we often have the money to do what we want.

Great, time and money—easy, right? The issue is that we usually don't know what we want to do. We have allowed ourselves to put our needs and dreams aside for so long it is hard to recall what they are.

I have a plan to get you back on track to stardom.

First and foremost, I believe that you need to find *the* dream.

Which dream? The dream that excites you, that fires you up that makes you want to get up in the morning. The dream you can't stop thinking about. If you don't know what it is, start to do some research. What do you like to do in your free time? Read, get together with friends, garden, travel? I would suggest tracking things that pique your interest and make you excited. We want the next chapter to be filled with joy and fun. It is up to you to define what that is for you.

Sometimes, there's an old dream we dust off, one that we always wanted and didn't dare say out loud. Maybe it's time to do that. Or maybe a new idea is growing. I suggest that whatever you are dreaming, make it bigger.

As you get more excited about your dream, you may find you want to tell someone. This can be tricky if you normally tell a close family member, as they might still be reeling from all the changes you made in their lives. They probably won't be the most receptive audience.

But don't get discouraged. Keep looking. Maybe in your friend group, another woman is in the same place in her life. It might even help to find a group of like-minded women that will be able to help you be the leading lady you are supposed to be.

There are groups out there that can really be supportive during this phase. I would look around your town, as I love in-person groups. You can connect more easily and feel their energy. Search for local women's groups online— Meet-ups is a great resource.

A few of my favorites are here. I love the Polka Dot Powerhouse, FemCity, and if you are ready to be an entrepreneur, eWomen Networks. They would benefit from your experience as you connect and share. Don't be afraid to get out there and introduce yourself. Share your dream and speak it into existence. Let your belief in yourself inspire others.

DECIDE

After you know what it is you want to create, you need to decide that you're going to do it. And I know that sounds easy. Just decide. Write a little note to yourself as a commitment. But it's very, very difficult for some people to decide to do it because it means change. And it means things are going to get uncomfortable for a little while.

I'll share a story with you. I had not realized how much I had dampened down my natural assertiveness when I remarried.

My husband is a wonderful man. I brought two beautiful little girls to our family. He has thoroughly enjoyed getting to be a father and looks forward to being a grandfather someday.

But what I realized as they got older, and we were living together for the first time without any children in the house, was that I started to be more assertive. It was a difficult, yearlong transition, as he basically had to get used to a new wife. It wasn't his fault. I realized that I had recast myself in a supporting role and created this situation.

But my assertiveness was a surprise to both of us. Because when you're a young mother with children, your first thought is to provide for and protect these children. And I realized by my behavioral changes, that's exactly what I was doing. I had been ensuring that there would be someone there in our lives to love and support us.

Then it hit me—I had been dimming my star instead of letting her shine her brightest light.

My point is deciding will not be easy for you, and deciding will not be easy for your family. But it is a necessary step for you to get to the life you want to lead.

You have your big dream, and you've decided you're going for it.

- You've written a note to yourself and posted it everywhere.
- You have shared this with someone who will be supportive and encouraging.
- You know you are a STAR.

DO.

Now it's time to do. That's my favorite part. Doing it is what I love.

But it may not be natural for you, and that's okay. If you're not sure how to start on the dream you want to pursue, talk to the ladies in your group, and feel free to reach out to me. Let's talk about the life you want to create. Join our retreat, created just for women like us.

This is where it gets particularly difficult for some of the people that love you because you're not acting as they expect. And even if they say they support you, understand they're still going to struggle with the new responsibilities you are passing to them and/or not doing for them anymore. Yes, it will be a transition. *But do not give up.*

What I can tell you as someone leading the way on this journey is this:

> *Doing is the most important part. This is where the transformation happens.*

> *This is where we take it out of the dream stage and move it into a reality.*

Once you've decided that this is the path you want to take, you must do the things that will move you to that life.

Action Items Recap:

Dream. Go buy a cute journal and start to jot down ideas as they come. Writing them down creates a connection with your brain and heart. Notice what makes you happy, brings you joy, or any ideas that just pop into your head that get you thinking. I suggest doing this for a few weeks to find out more about yourself.

Decide. For this step, I suggest doing at least these two things. One: Write a note to yourself that is a declaration of your intention to put your dream into action. Make a contract with yourself and sign and date it. If you would like to, post it on our Facebook page. Accountability is a key motivator. Two: Tell someone that can be an accountability buddy. This should be someone you trust to check up with you or motivate you. Maybe you can do this for each other. This is your promise to yourself.

Do: You can make the changes to lead you to a life you have been dreaming of living. Start with a few steps toward your goal. Baby steps still get you somewhere new. If you like To-Do lists, you can start one with simple first steps. Every action will lead to new experiences, new connections, and new opportunities. There will be no more waiting. You are making it happen.

You are the perfect woman to fulfill this role.

You are a STAR and leading lady.

I am glad and willing to be here to support you along the way and offer guidance. A leading lady should always know her role, and it's okay for you to take that role back. You are the star, and you deserve to be center stage in the spotlight. I see it already—your name in lights.

I know I met a wonderful woman when we started this chapter. But I am super excited to meet the leading lady you know you are. Welcome back to center stage.

PART
4

EMPOWER YOURSELF

W **HEN I STARTED** drafting the steps for my coaching framework, The Empowered Woman's Path, it became clear to me that, if self-empowerment was the end goal, it couldn't be where the path started. Before you empower yourself, there are a few required milestones that I have both outlined in my first book and that, now, the thirteen women who came before this part have beautifully described. Once you understand yourself better, you become aware of your imperfections and strengths and have the choice to embrace them and appreciate them all as an integral part of who you are— that's when you can finally take back your power. In my work of empowering myself and women, I came to the incredible conclusion that I am in the power seat—we all are. We are responsible for our happiness, success, and everything we desire for ourselves. This responsibility begins with controlling what we can control, and in the next few chapters, you will find individual stories and lessons from women who have done just that.

I connected with **Nina Macarie** in late 2018 in a virtual group for entrepreneurs when I saw her proposal to help business owners book more podcast interviews in exchange for some formal training. As I was just starting my business myself, I decided to reach out and give her a shot. Little did I know what would follow would be years of long-distance friendship and support, as we both grew our businesses. Nina's gentle spirit and powerful focus surprised me then and continues to surprise me now. In her chapter, she shares her side of the story and how she empowered herself to pursue her dreams and business by becoming more visible and encourages you to do the same.

Lorena Arnold and I met through a networking group and have bonded over so many commonalities, such as being immigrants in the US and having businesses that support women entrepreneurs. Her "grab-the-bull-by-its-horns" attitude and incredible life story of twists and turns embody the step of Empowering Yourself and present great encouragement for women who may be starting out on or continuing in their entrepreneurship journey.

A mutual friend connected **Pamela Maass Garrett** and me in 2020, so I could be interviewed on her podcast. Through the years, I watched Pam grow her family and her business and have been in awe of all she's accomplished. It was an honor to have her join this book to share her wisdom—not only as a mom and entrepreneur, but as an award-winning estate planning attorney in Colorado. She will empower you to control what you can, both in life and in death.

I knew of **Neha Naik** through entrepreneur friends in common, but it wasn't until we started working together in early 2023 that I could get a front-seat view of how much of a powerhouse she is. A mom, wife, and owner of several businesses, Neha outlines what exactly it takes to grow, run, and sustain a successful business, while wearing so many hats. Empowering is an understatement!

FROM SHY TO SHINING ON STAGES

By Nina Macarie

"**I WANNA BRING YOU** on my podcast, for sure."

"Yeah, I mean, thank you so much, but actually..."

"Would you be okay to be on it?"

"Um, the thing is that... yeah, I'm not sure. I don't know..."

"You get to decide."

This was part of my conversation with an entrepreneur and podcast host during a coffee chat back when I was still afraid of using my voice to share my message. I told her that I don't feel like I'm able to have a conversation that flows (even though we were having that conversation, right then). But a few months later, when I decided I was finally ready to do it, I went to check out her podcast, and surprisingly, she was no longer releasing new episodes. What a wasted opportunity.

You'd think this would be an opportunity that every entrepreneur would say "yes" to. But not me. Starting my business was a daunting task for me, plagued by self-doubt and a lack of confidence. I didn't realize what I was getting into. With a background in administration and having worked for the government in Romania, I believed my skills would naturally attract clients. My genuine intention was to assist fellow business moms in growing their ventures, as we all desired more time with our families while pursuing meaningful work. However, I soon discovered the challenges of self-promotion and selling my services.

In my late 30s, I embarked on this entrepreneurial journey, driven by a desire to escape the confines of a regular job. From a young age, I harbored grand ambitions of working in an international environment, particularly within the European Union. Growing up in a communist country until the age of 10, I remember my grandfather listening to "Radio Free" or "Radio Free Europe", which broadcasted stories of people defecting to Canada or the United States. Their bravery and the prospect of a better, freer life fascinated me.

Imagining the lives of people across borders captivated my curiosity. I pondered the differences between countries, the lives they led, their cuisine, and their leisure activities. Listening to those radio shows instilled in me a sense of possibility and expanded my vision beyond what seemed attainable. The stories I absorbed during that time played a more profound role in my life than I realized, shaping my decision-making process and providing strength during difficult moments.

I now understand why I have an affinity for podcasts. They allow my imagination to envision incredible possibilities that my eyes, alone, cannot perceive. As a dreamer, I have always coupled my aspirations with action, refusing to let my dreams wither or succumb to mediocrity.

Despite the obstacles and skeptics, I press on. I draw inspiration from the audacity of those who dared to pursue a better life, and I remain committed to helping others while achieving my own aspirations. By sharing my journey, listening to others' stories, and envisioning a future filled with boundless possibilities, I continue to navigate the entrepreneurial path with unwavering determination.

Just like (some of) you, I had moments where I felt stuck, wondering what to do next or why others could have success when I barely found a few clients to keep me above water. It's not that they are so different from you and me. Yes, some of them might be more gifted, more talented, but the thing that makes the difference is the drive, the desire to make it work no matter what. And if you want to treat your business like a business and not a hobby, it's your time to shine on stages so that more people learn about you and your amazing gifts.

Now, here is where I tell you how to move from shy to shining on stages using this simple, five-step framework: START.

S–Seek Clarity Through Action; T- Take Small Steps Toward Speaking Confidence; A–Amplify Your Courage for Greater Impact; R–Reach Out and Expand Opportunities; T–Tell Your Story to Inspire Others

SEEK CLARITY THROUGH ACTION

Clarity is often said to be achieved through action, and I couldn't agree more. When I started my business, my goal was to assist fellow entrepreneurial mothers in finding a balance between work and personal life. Initially, I lacked direction and struggled to secure long-term clients. However, I realized the importance of specialization and invested in various courses to enhance my skills. While I learned about Pinterest, sales funnels, and WordPress sites, I lacked the confidence to convince clients of my abilities. I believed that clients sought highly skilled freelancers, which discouraged me from taking action due to the perfectionism trap.

One day, I came across a masterclass on podcast pitching, which sparked my interest. Despite my self-doubt, I decided to reach out to a Facebook group, offering my services in exchange for the program. It may not seem a big deal to you, but to me, at that moment, it was huge. Marta Spirk, a remarkable business owner and mother of triplets, responded positively. Despite her initial reservations, she gave me a chance, leading to further opportunities and the experience I sought.

Marta's support contributed significantly to my growth as a business owner. Over time, I invested in additional courses and programs, including Marta's, which helped me gain the clarity I needed. Recognizing the value of audio, I realized what I wanted to be known for. This clarity became crucial for being featured on other platforms and sharing my story and expertise. By focusing on a specific area instead of trying to cover everything, I could differentiate myself from others and provide hosts with a compelling reason to invite me to their podcasts.

TAKE SMALL STEPS TOWARD SPEAKING CONFIDENCE

In the early stages of my business, I held the belief that being on stage was reserved for extroverted business owners or those unafraid of the spotlight. However, I made a conscious decision to become a braver and more courageous entrepreneur. This led to unexpected speaking opportunities that came my way without actively seeking them. Although, I still felt fear and uncertainty about speaking. I questioned my expertise and struggled to find my voice, despite gaining unique perspectives from working with clients and investing in programs.

To overcome these challenges, I began attending online networking events. Initially, I was hesitant and always introduced myself last in the breakout rooms. However, as I placed myself in situations that required me to speak, my confidence grew. A pivotal moment came when I learned about Marta's program, Shine Bright & CONNECT. Fed up with my excuses, I promptly joined, realizing that waiting for the perfect moment would only hinder my progress.

The icing on the cake was when Marta invited me to be featured in a video alongside two other spotlight students. Although nervous, saying yes was a proud moment. It provided me with tangible evidence that I was capable of speaking with confidence.

Consider the small steps you can take to improve your speaking skills, consistently. Participate in networking events, introduce yourself, and share your work. Record daily one-minute videos for social media or send voice messages to friends to grow comfortable with your own voice. Start with your network, even if they don't fully grasp your business. Seek support from online communities, find an accountability buddy, and connect with complementary business owners. Offer support to their audience and engage in coffee chats, which may lead to unexpected opportunities, like podcast interviews. Embrace small actions, such as Instagram takeovers or LinkedIn post swaps or email freebie swaps, that expose you to new audiences.

By taking these incremental steps, you'll gradually build speaking confidence and pave the way for greater success.

AMPLIFY YOUR COURAGE FOR GREATER IMPACT

While I had grown more comfortable with speaking, I still wasn't doing it regularly. I realized that I was using the excuse of investing in courses as a way to hide rather than take action. It was then that Marta unexpectedly approached me with an opportunity to host a masterclass on podcast pitching for her brand program. I was amazed by the serendipity and excited for the chance to work with Marta again. This time, I confidently said "yes" because I knew my topic well and believed I could provide valuable support to her clients in the realm of podcast pitching.

From my perspective, amplifying courage means actively seeking opportunities that push you beyond your comfort zone and encourage boldness. We often believe we need more courses or programs before we're ready. We procrastinate and make excuses due to fear of judgment, failure, rejection, or the unknown. We think we're not famous or successful enough, so we wait months or even years to grow our businesses, while others seize opportunities without second-guessing themselves. We underestimate the value of our common skills or experiences, assuming they're uninteresting to others. However, what may seem ordinary to us could be fascinating to someone else who wants to learn from our journey, perspectives, and lessons.

When someone discovers us and needs our product or service, they are likely interested in our beginnings, motivations, and the process we refined. Details we might consider boring could be intriguing to them because they want to delve deeper into our expertise.

Sharing your message and mission across different platforms and audiences requires courage. What is the number one fear you want to overcome next? Remember, make your dreams bigger than your fears. Embrace the courage to share your story, insights, and experiences to inspire and impact others.

REACH OUT AND EXPAND OPPORTUNITIES

Reaching out to others and seeking collaboration can be intimidating. I understand that feeling all too well. I still remember the first time I approached a potential podcast pitching client and received my first rejection. It hit me personally, and I needed a couple of days to gather the courage to inform my client. However, it's important to remember that a "no" doesn't always reflect a rejection of yourself (unless your pitch was poorly executed). Most often, it's simply part of their selection process. For podcasts with weekly episodes, they only have a limited number of spots available, considering they also have other desired guests. So, if they receive 10 pitches in a week, they can only say "yes" to one out of 10.

That's why starting with your network and consistently reaching out to people is crucial. Not only do you feel more confident engaging with familiar individuals, but you also strengthen your outreach skills. When you eventually send cold pitches or reach out to industry leaders and complementary businesses, you'll have the evidence and confidence to know that you already possess what it takes.

Approaching others with a genuine interest in exploring your mission, rather than solely focusing on a transactional exchange, will profoundly impact your presence, message delivery, and connection with hosts and their audiences. Podcast guesting, in my opinion, serves as the foundational level to enhance your confidence, refine your message, and gain visibility, ultimately propelling you to new heights. It becomes a springboard for even greater visibility opportunities, such as appearing on TV, delivering a TEDx talk, writing a book, or hosting your own event (online or offline).

When you record a podcast interview, it's like sitting across from a friend. By that point, you should have familiarized yourself with them through social media, their website, and their previous episodes. It becomes an intimate conversation, and once you're comfortable at this stage, you'll be ready to spread your wings and soar to new levels in your business.

By nurturing relationships, expanding your network, and leveraging podcast guesting as a starting point, you'll gain the confidence and momentum needed to achieve extraordinary growth and impact in your entrepreneurial journey.

TELL YOUR STORY TO INSPIRE OTHERS

There's no better way to connect with your audience than by sharing your story repeatedly in front of new audiences. I discovered that the more I practiced, the more comfortable I became with showing up. However, I noticed that, while I felt at ease sharing my expertise, I struggled with opening up and sharing my personal story. As an introvert, I found it challenging to reveal myself and share personal details.

Everything changed for me when I made a decision at the end of last year. I committed to saying "yes" to every opportunity that would contribute to my personal and professional growth in 2023. This mindset shift led me to two incredible opportunities: being part of this book and participating in an immersive program called the Break in Spain, funded by the European Union.

The program exceeded all expectations. Initially, I was a bit disappointed that I wouldn't be spending my time in a big city but in a village. However, living in an Andalusian village for three weeks transformed my life completely. Surrounded by nearly 20 European women entrepreneurs, along with mentors and facilitators, I reconnected with myself, reflected on my grand vision, and found myself in situations I never thought possible. I delivered my first in-person presentation on my passion, podcast guesting. I was interviewed by a local Spanish TV station. I even presented our collective project, developed during the program, to the village mayor and locals. These were opportunities I believed were reserved for others, and I, initially, resisted them. However, I learned to embrace them, realizing they were meant to teach me valuable lessons, demonstrate my capabilities, and inspire others through leading by example.

These experiences gave me the strength to persevere, even during moments when I wanted to quit or felt a deep sense of loneliness (a feeling many solopreneurs can relate to). We all have stories to share, as we've all faced challenges, hardships, and difficulties. The moment we decide to take a step forward, initiate change without blaming others, and hold ourselves accountable, we unleash the power within us. If you're tired of playing small and feeling stuck, these moments become catalysts for a new and empowered version of yourself.

So, embrace your story, embrace your growth, and share it boldly. Your experiences have the potential to inspire, motivate, and connect with others on a profound level.

IT IS ABOUT TIME

By Lorena Arnold

*C*AN I CONFESS something to you?

When I founded my company, the Women on FIRE Academy, and first started working with entrepreneurs and real estate investors, I hated it. I thought I would enjoy it, but I quickly realized I hated it—though, I love it now.

Back then, I felt the life being sucked out of me. Most depressing was the thought that I had walked away from, by many people's standards, a "dream corporate job" where I had the prestige, respect, and power to start this venture. And, lo and behold, I hated it.

It occurred to me that, maybe, I had made a mistake.

You might ask, what was I doing before the FIRE academy?

Let me take you back—all the way back. To understand why I hated working with entrepreneurs in this new business that I had founded—the same one that I now love—it would probably help if you knew a thing or two about me. Not on a business level, but on a personal level.

The year was 2008. Financially speaking, I had just received the life insurance of my deceased husband. It took a year after his death, struggling and suffering over money, before the check finally arrived. I was 45 years old, and all of a sudden, I had more money than my parents ever had. Up to that point, I had never held more than $5,000 in savings in my bank account, as we always had the big expenses—mortgage, car loans, credit cards, and no budget to account for it all. So, this was a big change. I literally thought I was rich, which reveals just how naïve and foolish I was with money.

The breakthrough for me, though, that led to this turnaround—which is what you're probably most interested in—was discovering a new money mindset, a new relationship with money.

A few years before this, back in 2003, I was divorced and trying to make ends meet by working in a corporate job and starting my real estate investments. I was broke. I was also depressed. I'm not going to lie, I never intended to be living the life I am now—as an author, entrepreneur, and business coach.

From an early age, I wanted to be a concert pianist, following my grandmother's famous sister. However, my parents had other plans for me, and back then, following a computer science degree was the right thing to do to keep my parents happy.

This journey led me to continue my higher education in the United States, which also made my parents happy, as they were sending me away from a very close relationship with my then-boyfriend. Needless to say, I quickly replaced that relationship with another guy, marrying young and having two toddlers before my 25th birthday. Our marriage lasted 18 years before I was faced with a long and contentious divorce.

But I continued my education. I graduated, got the corporate job, met another guy, and we got married shortly thereafter. However, I did not know I would face his devastating death in less than a year.

This led to depression again.

I felt like everything I had worked for had been yanked out from underneath me. During this low point of my life, I lost the house I couldn't afford, the car, the furniture, and well as the corporate job I worked so hard to keep. But that also inspired me to change.

It was time. Something needed to change. I could no longer rely on a corporate job or on a husband or even my parents to support me financially.

In order to make ends meet, pay the bills, and be able to buy Christmas presents for my boys, I got my real estate license and started buying and selling real estate in May of that year. The checks were small at the beginning, but they served their purpose, providing me with a little extra cash to get by.

Then, something happened. I received a present—a book that would dramatically change my life. I don't really believe in fate. I am not a religious person, and I was not very spiritual back then. But something—the universe—intervened. I had never taken a money mindset class in my life. I had no experience with big money, and frankly, I wasn't all that interested in creating my own business. I honestly thought this whole "real estate" thing would just be a year or two gig until I found another corporate job. But then, a book fell into my hands.

That book was *Rich Woman* by Kim Kiyosaki.

For whatever reason, it fascinated me. As I flipped through the pages, it talked about women and their relationship with money and how it was time for women to take control of their finances without being told what to do.

I felt inspired and motivated. I had never read a book with such conviction about money or financial independence, and I began to think that I could do it, too. I certainly did not want to lose sleep over money again. Instead, I wanted to take control of my financial future so that I would no longer have to look for a rich prince charming. I demanded true independence.

Long story short, her book changed my life. I know that sounds like a cliché, and if you own the book, then you know that it's a fairly basic book for real estate investing—nothing too advanced or sophisticated.

But I have a very addictive personality, and that book provided me with my first "taste". I became obsessed—not just with real estate but also with the behavior of money.

Everything was going great.

After a miserable first year in real estate, I was now making a nice six-figure income. But, there was a problem. I didn't really care about real estate. I wasn't passionate about real estate. It paid the bills, sure. It provided me with a certain, very comfortable, lifestyle, but it didn't fascinate me.

My love affair was with money. I call him "Mr. Money", last name "Wealth". Because of this new love affair, I started neglecting my real estate business to study the art, language, personality, and behavior of Mr. Money.

I shut down my real estate business, deciding to become a money breakthrough business coach. A money breakthrough business coach is not a financial planner and won't ever tell you what to do with your money. In my coaching, I focus on women and money.

When I started, I'm not sure I even knew what a money coach was; I just knew I wanted to learn to help women build a better relationship with money. Further, I decided If I was going to do this, I wanted to study with and learn from the best in the world. At the top of my list was an award-winning small business expert, Kendall Summerhawk.

She asked me to write a letter about my thoughts and beliefs regarding money. In the letter, I stated what I wanted was for women to never lose sleep over money again, for women to take control of their financial futures, and for women to demand true financial independence.

These were the ideas that started me down this path.

As a money breakthrough business coach, I work on my own time, which is a type of freedom I want for the women I coach. I believe women should not depend on a partner, parents, corporate job, pension, or social security. I coach women to build their businesses and get paid what they are worth, finding their unique brilliance, and having a better relationship with their money—yes, dating "Mr. Money", last name "Wealth".

As I learned more, I discovered old, limiting beliefs about money I was carrying from my parents, from my childhood, that unconsciously prevented me from having the success I really wanted. I thought, "How can I help others if I, myself, need help?"

Here is the thing: I decided that what I didn't know but needed to know, I would learn. I would buy books, go to the library, contact and interview experts to pick their brains, or in this case, ask to be pointed in the direction of the money expert. In order to learn what I needed to know to understand money, I required access to the art of money.

So, I researched and Googled books about money and who inspired me the most. Who were the "woman" money people? And I wasn't talking just financial—like Suzan Orman or Dave Ramsey. I wanted more inspirational money behavior, the emotional, psychological, and spiritual behavior around money, including my own beliefs and myths that surrounded it.

Something, again, I learned from Kim Kiyosaki was that you need to study the biggest winners. You need to look for the commonalities. You need to break down their mental process and look for repeated themes and storylines.

That's what I did. I deconstructed the biggest winners.

In other words, I didn't need to fix my own money mindset before I could fix other people's mindsets. Becoming a money breakthrough business coach helped me identify what I needed to understand about money to help others, as well—to successfully help others manifest prosperity and create their life's work using abundance techniques, positive affirmations, and learning to master money in their lives.

I wanted to be the best, and I was willing to do anything to achieve it.

I didn't shut down a six-figure real estate business just to be "okay".

During this time of self-discovery, I deconstructed money and the philosophy of it, the behavior of it, and the archetypes of it. I mapped out a strategy for how to teach about money—and that is how the Women on FIRE Academy was formed.

I have started two other businesses with the same concept of building a money mindset. And it all starts with understanding "what is money for"—that is precisely the core of my program, to teach women entrepreneurs the understanding of what is money for by applying a three-tier mastering of money mindset by using MBA—money mindset, body/branding, action, and acknowledgment.

You don't master money by learning one or two cheap secrets.

You have to be obsessed.

You have to be willing to deconstruct your money mindset, so that when those big ideas reveal themselves, you can spot the repeated themes and storylines.

Your relationship with money determines your level of business success or failure.

When I first founded my company, the reason I hated it was that every business owner I spoke to, every investor I spoke to, had no idea what they wanted money for. They knew they wanted it now, and they wanted it a lot, but they didn't know why. And they couldn't see the blocks in their own money mindset that were keeping them from earning what they were worth.

If this is your first introduction to me, and my beliefs, my way of thinking about business and money—about living your life's mission and purpose—then I hope I have made a good first impression.

Above all, I hope that I have ignited your imagination to consider what's really possible for you and your business when you allow yourself to embrace your vision and refuse to be ordinary.

PLANNING FOR YOU DEATH EMPOWERS YOU TO IMPROVE YOUR LIFE

By Pamela Maass Garrett

"*I* CAN'T WAIT FOR you to get started!" I beamed, the smile leaping from my face as I eagerly greeted Sarah, my first employee! Sarah had just accepted my offer to join the new business I was launching.

I then read the contract for a three-year lease on a new, larger office space—two large offices with the option to add more over the coming months. My vision for my new business included happy clients coming to our office and almost dancing as they left. I could see our happy team growing, and I would order a huge, bright white name plaque for our lobby.

My entire life savings were invested into launching my law firm, and to top it all off, I had just discovered I was pregnant. Okay. It was fine—wonderful, even! I felt like everything in my life was falling into place. Life was Good!

Then I turned on the television. It was March 2020—the world was shutting down due to the Covid-19 pandemic. My heart sank. My dreams were dying. Fear gripped me. My pregnancy hormones were not helpful at this moment, and I felt shattered. How would I meet with clients during a shutdown? My business relied on in-person meetings. How would I support my family? How would we pay the mortgage? How would I take time off to take care of my new baby? I had put all my money into launching this firm. Years of planning, saving, and working hard—vaporized. Oh no! And what about Sarah? How would I pay Sarah, my new employee who had just given up her job at a large firm to take a chance with my startup law firm?

I had fallen from a confident founder to feeling like a scared little girl again... and I was about to become a mother.

But I had to be the strong, confident founder—for myself and for my daughter. I had to become the "Law Mother". Oftentimes, our deepest problems become opportunities. I was not in this pandemic alone. Nor was I the only person coming to face difficult realities.

What I would realize in the coming weeks was that the global pandemic wasn't the death of my business but the spark to transform my business, my life, and the lives of my clients. As an estate planning attorney, the pandemic forced my clients and I to face life, health, and death in a very real and personal way.

The realizations and risks we faced in the pandemic led to three important lessons that we can all carry forward to improve our lives.

First, when we feel vulnerable and powerless, when there are threats and uncertainties, when events outside our control threaten our family and our livelihoods, controlling the controllable gives us peace of mind.

Second, people think they fear death, but death seems rather remote and abstract to most of us. Yes, we do have a related fear—but what we actually fear is that we are not really living our lives to the fullest.

Third, planning for your death improves your life. Accepting that you will eventually die and then deliberately planning for your death allows you to face deeper fears—beyond death. Once we accept the inevitability of death, and face the current and future realities, we are *empowered*. We can prioritize what's important in our lives, what's important for those we care about, and we can live life to the fullest.

Rather than the pandemic suppressing demand for our services, my law firm phone was flooded with more calls than ever. People who had put off setting up their wills or trusts for years were now faced with the threat of a global pandemic and saw the very real possibility of death. They wanted some control, so they chose to put a plan in place.

For example: One client worried that if they were hospitalized, their loved ones wouldn't be able to visit them because of the quarantine and would not be able to help them with end-of-life decisions. Even though clients couldn't control the world around them or the pandemic, they felt relieved the moment they signed their estate planning documents. Empowered, they had control over decisions in a worst-case scenario.

I felt this same sense of relief when I gave birth to my daughter. In the middle of the night, I woke up to alarms sounding with nurses and doctors rushing into my hospital room. Our vitals had taken a turn for the worse.

Fortunately, the medical staff were wonderful, and 12 hours later, my baby girl was safely cuddling in my arms.

When the alarms had gone off, I was afraid we may not make it. I didn't think much about mortality before I became a mother. But when I would leave my little girl to go to work, fear crept in. The first time I left for a business trip, I worried about what would happen to my daughter and my husband if I died. As an estate planning attorney, though, I had a full plan in place and good life insurance. And though the fear and sadness were still there, I felt a little more peaceful knowing that they would always be taken care of, no matter what.

The second lesson I learned is that people fear something deeper than death. In my law practice, I spoke with hundreds of families during the pandemic, and I discovered my clients were afraid of something else.

A couple I worked with couldn't decide who they should name as guardians to their young daughters. They had a challenging situation—the wife's parents and siblings were drug addicts and alcoholics. The husband was an only child, and his parents were too old to raise children.

The wife had a good friend but worried that raising her two girls seemed like too much to ask of her. As the husband started sharing possible other names, the wife screamed out, "This is exactly why I have been putting off estate planning! I wish we had better families and closer connections!"

I had previously believed that Americans culturally avoid talking about death. These clients helped me see it was something deeper. Facing her death made her think about what was truly missing from her life—connections and community. This insight was transformational for her. When she realized what was really bothering her, she was able to move forward and address it.

This led to the third lesson: By planning for death, you face your actual fears and discover what you are truly missing in your life.

I asked the wife to reach out to her friend and then to get back to me.

A few weeks later, she called me back. She happily reported that her friend felt honored to fill the role of guardian for her daughters. After her phone call, her friend began taking a more active role in their daughters' lives. The experience of creating their estate plan led her and her husband to nurture their sense of community, to become more involved with their church, and to build stronger relationships with their friends.

I noticed a similar pattern with other clients. Clients think about their death and then identify aspects of their life they want to improve. For example, I have observed divorced fathers reconnecting with their children, seniors building new relationships, and families spread across the country reconnecting.

The next time you worry about your death, I invite you to take the first step and control the controllable. An easy way to get started with your estate plan is to just collect a list of everything you own and share this with someone you love. Without this, your loved ones would have to search through all your mail, computer files, and records to try and determine everything you have. This frustrating process can take years, and assets can, sometimes, be lost.

Second, I invite you to think about who would need your protection if you were to pass away today. If you are married, is everything set up to pass to your partner smoothly? If you have children, who would you trust to take care of them? Are the assets you are leaving behind enough to take care of your spouse and children, or are you going to leave them in a hardship?

Third, as you go through the process above, ask yourself: If I died today, what would I regret missing out on in my life? What do I want to prioritize and address to live my life more fully?

My law firm did not collapse during the pandemic. In our darkest hour, we faced our deepest fears, as did our clients. As a result, we helped more families than ever protect their loved ones and transform their lives. We spent two years helping clients virtually from our homes. Today, we are a team of seven, stronger through overcoming adversity, and we finally moved into our dream office with the bright white name plaque in our lobby.

Remember, when we feel vulnerable, controlling the controllable gives us peace of mind. What we fear more than death is not truly living our lives to the fullest. And finally, planning for our death empowers us to examine what's truly important and improve our lives.

DELEGATING YOUR WAY TO SUCCESS

By Neha Naik

*H*AVING DROPPED OUT of medical school, the pressure to succeed was more intense than ever. I was driven by a deep-seated fear of failure and a desire to contribute to my family's finances. Yet, I had grand dreams, not just of business success but of becoming the best version of myself in all my roles. As Neha Naik, I wanted to excel as a mother, be a supportive and caring wife, and also stand as a remarkable business owner. This ambition propelled me to quit my full-time job and start my recruiting agency, where I help startups scale. In the beginning, it was just a few clients. But soon, word-of-mouth recommendations led to more and more clients coming in—and I didn't want to turn them away! I wanted to continue building the momentum, and in doing so, I was trying to do it all by myself.

Pretty quickly, I realized that the reality of juggling these roles was exhausting, pushing me to my limits. In my quest for excellence, I learned a crucial lesson about delegation. As the founder of a recruitment agency on the cusp of scaling, I discovered that letting go and trusting others to share my workload was a critical step in my journey. It not only aided the growth and success of my business but also allowed me to make strides toward becoming the mom, wife, and entrepreneur I aspired to be.

I vividly recall the overwhelming exhaustion that came with juggling the roles of both a mother and an entrepreneur. My early mornings were a chaotic blend of tending to my little ones and preparing for the workday. As the day progressed, I was consumed by a whirlwind of responsibilities, from tending to client meetings and deadlines to the various domestic tasks waiting at home. The nights were particularly grueling, as I found myself in front of my computer, sifting through a deluge of emails, slack messages, and unfinished work. The constant tug-of-war between my dual roles as a mom and businesswoman was draining, pushing me to the edge of a breakdown. The guilt of seemingly failing in both realms gnawed at me incessantly, adding to my growing stress.

My breaking point arrived one gloomy night, alone in my office, drowning in a sea of unpaid invoices, unanswered emails, and missed family events. Doubts and fears clawed at my mind, with thoughts like, "Am I good enough?" and "Have I taken on more than I can handle?". In that clarity, I recognized I was spiraling into a cycle of burnout. The toughest part was acknowledging my own limitations and the missed moments with loved ones. I took a leap of faith, delegating tasks that once seemed inseparable from my identity. By seeking support and offloading responsibilities, I wasn't just preserving my energy and joy but also embracing the truth that going solo wasn't the answer.

As I began to delegate, I experienced a transformative shift in my life and work. My business began to flourish, and I found a semblance of balance that had previously seemed elusive. The act of delegating allowed me to be more present for my children and focus on aspects of my business that truly required my attention and expertise. The realization that asking for help and trusting others with important tasks wasn't a sign of weakness but rather an embodiment of strength and wisdom was a game-changer.

LETTING GO

Because you're so personally connected to your business, it's natural to feel scared about handing off essential tasks to someone else. The fear of letting go is akin to dropping off your precious baby at daycare or leaving them with a nanny for the first time. I know this feeling all too well.

I can vividly recall the emotions that coursed through me on that momentous day when I had to part with my little one. Doubts plagued my mind as I questioned every decision I had made leading up to that point. Was I doing the right thing? Would my child be okay without me? It felt as if nobody else could care for my baby as well as I could. I grappled with a profound sense of unease, wondering if I was making a grave mistake.

As a business owner, those same apprehensions resurfaced when I contemplated delegating tasks to others. The thought of entrusting someone else with the intricate knowledge and understanding I had of my business was daunting. The words echoed in my mind: "Nobody else knows this business like I do." It seemed easier to shoulder the burden myself, believing that if I couldn't do everything, I was, somehow, failing.

That fear, that belief that we must do it all, is a trap that ensnares many business owners. We fall into the false notion that our worth is tied to our ability to handle every aspect of our business, single-handedly. We convince ourselves that relinquishing control is a sign of weakness, a betrayal of our dedication.

But here's the truth—we cannot scale our businesses if we don't let go. Even Jeff Bezos, the mastermind behind Amazon, started small, personally delivering packages door-to-door to cut costs. Yet, he knew that for his business to truly soar, he had to find a way to scale it. You won't find him driving around neighborhoods today, tirelessly delivering boxes. He understood the power of delegation and focused his energy on steering Amazon into the global giant it has become.

If you, like me, have been gripped by the fear of letting go, I want you to know that I see you. I understand the terror that accompanies the mere thought of relinquishing control. It feels like surrendering a piece of ourselves, a piece of our dreams.

But it's time to confront reality. To scale our businesses, to achieve the success we envision, we must shed our fears and embrace the power of delegation. We must recognize that giving up tasks and responsibilities that don't require our personal touch is not a failure. It's a strategic move that frees up our time and energy to focus on the bigger picture, on the aspects of our business that truly demand our attention.

Just as we trust capable hands to care for our children, we must trust in the abilities of others to support our business growth. It won't be easy. It will require vulnerability and relinquishing control. But as we learn to delegate, we'll discover a newfound freedom, a path to scalability and success that we couldn't have achieved on our own.

So, take that leap of faith. Release the grip on tasks that drain you and watch as your business blossoms. Embrace the transformative power of delegation and allow yourself to soar to new heights. Remember, you are not failing by letting go; you are propelling yourself toward a future where your business thrives, and you find the balance you deserve.

THE CHALLENGE OF SMALL BUSINESS OWNERSHIP AND SCALING

Getting past that hump of going from a five- to a six-figure small business is incredibly challenging without delegating tasks. I know this firsthand because I found myself trapped in that very struggle, desperately trying to juggle the demands of my growing business while maintaining a semblance of quality and sanity.

As my business started to gain momentum, I found myself facing a waitlist of clients, each one eager for their project to be completed. But the truth was, I couldn't keep up with the workload. There simply weren't enough hours in the day to meet everyone's expectations. Time became my enemy, relentlessly ticking away as I scrambled to finish the never-ending stream of tasks.

With the mounting pressure, I soon discovered that the quality of my work began to suffer. I was spread thin, frantically trying to fill orders, but in doing so, I couldn't devote the necessary time and attention to each project. It was a painful realization—one that left me feeling defeated and questioning my abilities as a business owner.

Inevitably, the consequences hit me hard. Clients started looking elsewhere, seeking faster turnaround times or superior quality work. It was a double blow—losing revenue and losing trust. I found myself trapped in a cycle of constant busyness, struggling to stay afloat while my dreams of a thriving, successful business slipped further away.

If you're going through this, I understand the depths of your frustration and fear. I've stood in those shoes, feeling the weight of disappointment and the relentless pressure to keep up. The thought of delegating tasks and responsibilities may seem terrifying, as if you're relinquishing control over the very essence of your business.

But here's the truth: You didn't embark on this entrepreneurial journey to work 70 hours a week and still worry about hitting your revenue targets. You didn't sacrifice the stability of a full-time job for endless stress and sleepless nights. No, you took the leap because you craved freedom—the freedom to control your own schedule, to have time for your passions and your loved ones.

Ironically, it's the controlling spirit that brought you here that now holds you back. To break free from the cycle and reach the six-figure milestone, you must embrace the power of delegation. It's a necessary step, one that will allow you to focus on the core aspects of your business and reclaim the freedom you yearned for when you started this journey.

Yes, it's scary to let go, to entrust others with tasks that feel so deeply intertwined with your business. But by doing so, you open up space for growth, for the pursuit of excellence, and for the creation of a sustainable, thriving enterprise. Delegating isn't a sign of weakness—it's an act of courage, a strategic move that propels you toward the success you've always envisioned.

So, take that leap of faith, my fellow entrepreneur. Break free from the chains of overwork and diminishing returns. Embrace the art of delegation, and watch as your business not only reaches new heights but also affords you the freedom and fulfillment you set out to achieve. You deserve it.

HOW I FINALLY LET GO OF THE CONTROL FREAK INSIDE OF ME

Like many business owners and founders, I consider myself Type A. I like to have control over everything in my life. I went into business for myself because I wanted to have more control over my schedule and the work I did. I didn't want to be bossed around—I wanted to be my own boss.

So, when I first started thinking about delegating tasks for my businesses, I panicked. As in, literal panic attacks.

I had crazy thoughts centered around one question: "What am I *doing*?"

I felt like I was cheating on my business. Was it worth going behind my business's back for a little breathing room? But I knew that something had to give. I was running three businesses, raising two kids, being a wife, a daughter, a daughter-in-law, while staying healthy and trying to do all the other things that needed to be done around the house and in my life.

So, I finally took a breath and let go.

My first two hires were by far the most challenging. They were the ones that tested my strength and trust as a business owner.

Once I settled into my new normal of not doing everything for my business, I felt relief. Instead of spending several hours a week sending invoices, following up on emails, and doing all those other small tasks that add up to huge time-sinks, I could really settle in and focus on my area of expertise.

Guess what happened?

My businesses *grew*. Once I had more time to strategize, I could scale my businesses so they could continue growing. Now, I'm making more money and doing less work than I was before I started hiring employees.

I currently have a team of almost 45 people. Having an entire staff of employees means I get to enjoy my life. I can go to the gym in the middle of the afternoon and be at home for my kids when they get home, at night and on the weekends. I don't have to spend all weekend working while my family either does fun stuff without me or sits around and waits for me to finish "just this one thing" (which, we all know, is never "just one thing").

STARTING SMALL

I firmly believe that who we are at work mirrors who we are at home.

You're not going to be a control freak at work and utterly lackadaisical at home.

Chances are, if you're having a hard time letting go of tasks at work, you are also the type of person who believes you are the only one who can do certain things at home. And you probably get annoyed when someone else does them because they don't do them exactly how you would.

Yeah, I see you. So, here's something I want you to try.

Think about everything you do to support your family and household during a given day. Now, think about which of those things could be easily done by someone else.

I'll go first.

My kids are three and six years old.

It's easier and faster for me to pick out what my six-year-old wears daily. I can go into his closet, choose an outfit, help put it on, and boom, we're out the door. It takes much longer to let him pick out his clothes and painstakingly put them on himself—especially the shoes. Does anyone else's kid take *forever* to put on their shoes? It can't just be mine.

Anyway, that's an example of something I learned to let go of. I know it will take longer to let him get dressed before we leave for school, so I just set aside a few extra minutes to ensure we're not late.

And guess what?

Once he gets the hang of getting dressed on his own, my life will become a lot easier. That'll free a few minutes for me to finish getting the three-year-old ready, chat with my spouse, or take an extra sip of coffee while it's hot.

You don't need to have kids for this to work.

Say you're always the one who does the laundry. Let your partner do it for a change! Or the dishes, or making dinner, or buying groceries. Try an online grocery delivery service or cleaning service and trust that the person who does your shopping or cleaning will do a good job. The goal is to let go of the feeling that you are *the only one* who can manage a particular task.

I know that this might seem like extra work upfront. I also know that how you're living isn't how you want to be living. You don't want to be working 80 hours a week on your business, then doing everything around the house in your personal life. That's not why you started a business!

So, start small. Find one thing that you can delegate to someone else. Think about it right now. And as soon as you put this chapter down, go and delegate that task. I don't care how small it is. It could be taking the garbage out, putting the laundry in the dryer, making dinner, or picking that random piece of trash off the floor that everyone else in the household seems all too happy to ignore.

One thing. Start with one thing. Then, add another thing next week. I want you to start thinking of tasks to delegate until you are delegating at least one thing a day.

As you think of things to delegate, consider who to delegate them to, and set your expectations accordingly. For example, it's probably not a great idea to delegate laundry duty to a four-year-old and expect immaculate results. But your four-year-old is probably more than capable of picking up pieces of trash that have accumulated around the house.

While you move through your week of delegation, I want you to think about how much lighter you feel when you don't have to be the person managing it all. Don't worry about how someone else is going to do it. Trust that the person you are delegating the task to has the means to do it without ruining everything.

As a determined and visionary woman CEO, recognizing the weight of responsibilities is crucial. Begin by distinguishing tasks—identify what only you can accomplish, understand those that are important but can be delegated, and address the tasks you may have been setting aside. Prioritization is not just about managing time, but also about maximizing your unique skill set and perspective.

Setting ambitious revenue goals is a testament to your capabilities and aspirations. Growth and progress, both personal and organizational, come from pushing beyond the familiar. By setting benchmarks that challenge you, you are not only expanding your company's horizons but also reaffirming your dynamic role as a leader.

Hiring and delegating shouldn't be seen as relinquishing control but as strategic scaling. Whether you're considering W-2 employees, freelancers, or third-party agencies, trust is paramount. Trust in the potential of your hires, and more importantly, trust in your judgment and ability to lead and inspire. Remember, leadership is as much about empowering others as it is about directing the path forward.

I will leave you with this final thought.

Before entrusting tasks to others in your business, first learn to trust and prioritize yourself. When you're stretched thin between work, family, and personal needs, self-care often falls by the wayside. Begin by setting small, achievable personal goals, like eating healthier or incorporating daily exercise. This self-trust not only improves your well-being but paves the way for delegating and scaling your business. By stepping back and focusing on the bigger picture, you allow your venture to reach new heights.

So, get out there and start delegating your way to success!

PART

5

TRANSFORM YOURSELF

*T*RANSFORMATION GOES BEYOND our personal lives; it encompasses our surroundings and can even make an impact on the whole world. My goal when developing The Empowered Woman's Path was to start transformation, one woman at a time, in order to touch their families, clients, and spread through their communities and cities. By now, I hope this book has helped you see that transformation has nothing to do with becoming a different person, but rather becoming more accepting of who you've been and already are, so you can lead your purest authentic life and encourage others to do the same. In this fifth and final part, you will find truly transformational stories that shed light on impossible situations that required extreme resilience, support, and self-trust.

I met **Delaney Jensen-Hager** through her mother, another contributor to this book, Vesta Hager. Since her mom and I have become good friends, it made sense that

Delaney and I would resonate with each other, too. As a mom myself, to much younger kids, I see their relationship as something I aspire to have with my children—especially my daughter. Learning about Delaney's challenges and how Vesta has not only supported her but encouraged her to pursue her path is inspiring. In her chapter, she talks about a rocky road toward her dyslexia diagnosis, managing her conditions, and now using her voice for awareness.

Denise Bruschi and I were introduced by another author in this book, Lorena Arnold, as we were beginning the project. Her strength while facing various life challenges is remarkable and makes for an important contribution in this part of the book, as well as in using your voice to advocate for yourself.

Patricia Dieudonne came into my world through a mutual connection in early 2023, and her lively personality resonated with me immediately. Later, as we got to work together to craft her signature talk, I learned about her life story and challenges and became even more inspired by her. In her chapter, she outlines how not once, but twice, a terrifying diagnosis encouraged her to transform her life and dedicate her time and business to empowering others to do the same.

Much like the previous ladies in this part, **Karleen Wagner**'s sweet spirit and light approach to life would never give away the amount of hardship she's been through. I have been blessed to connect with her more personally in 2023, after knowing her for a few years, and she closes off this part and book with personal lessons of transformation that anyone can identify themselves with.

SUPERWOMAN:
DELANEY THE DYSLEXIC

By Delaney Jensen-Hager

HE QUIXKG BROWNS foxe jumps over the lzay dog. The quick brown fox jumps over the lazy dog. Now, you'll notice the two versions of that sentence are different. The first sentence is how I, someone with dyslexia, experience it. I see the same sentence but with letters that don't belong and letters that are in the wrong spots. That's how I see everything. Every piece of paper that's handed to me looks like that sentence. Every paper I write looks like that sentence. For years, it scared me that my sentences look different from everybody else's, but I realized something: my sentences may look different, but being different isn't a bad thing. That just makes me unique. As soon as I noticed that I was uniquely me, I realized that I probably wasn't the only one feeling worried about my differences, so I made it my mission to teach the world about my story and how living with dyslexia makes life exciting.

I spent a lot of my life scared of an official diagnosis. It didn't get better right away once I got the diagnosis, either.

I was diagnosed with dyslexia, dysgraphia, dyspraxia, dyscalculia, generalized anxiety disorder, test anxiety, and obsessive-compulsive disorder (OCD). All of these words are terrifying, I get it. I thought if I had to walk around with the labels "dyslexic", "anxious", and "OCD" attached to me for the rest of my life that it would become my Kryptonite, a weakness that I didn't know how to control, or if I even could. Now that I have had time to reflect on my diagnosis and have had years to live with it, it doesn't scare me anymore. I figured out how my brain works, how to not only manage this fear but harness the power of fear and make it my superpower. It took me years to do that, but I learned the foundation for those skills because of school.

When it came to the world after I graduated, I thought this diagnosis would continue to be my Kryptonite, but getting that diagnosis gave me a purpose. It gave me a mission to ensure that nobody else ever feels like I did. It gave me a reason to look into what it means to have dyslexia. I found who I was by getting diagnosed. Going through the process and getting a diagnosis is terrifying, and there isn't anything that anyone can say to you that makes it less terrifying. Regardless, my goal, my hope, my mission is to make sure nobody else feels as terrified as I did because you have someone in your corner now: Me.

I want to be your biggest cheerleader. I want to be your biggest resource. I want to be the reason you start sharing your story, too. Learning that you have dyslexia will be scary, but it shouldn't prevent you from taking charge of your life. It shouldn't make you live in a place of fear. What it should do is empower you, and that's what we're here to talk about.

So, what exactly is dyslexia? The National Institute of Neurological Disorders and Stroke defines dyslexia as a learning disability that impairs a person's ability to read.[8] The Mayo Clinic includes common characteristics, such as difficulty with spelling, the manipulation of sound, and rapid visual-verbal responding.[9] There's no set treatment for dyslexia because it affects each brain uniquely. No one knows what happens because the brain is still so unknown. On top of dyslexia, I also have dyspraxia, dysgraphia, and dyscalculia. Those with dyslexia struggle with reading. Those with dyspraxia have trouble with physical coordination. Those with dysgraphia struggle with writing, spelling, and putting thoughts on paper. Lastly, those with dyscalculia struggle with numbers and math.

"Dyslexia can be hard to diagnose because there is no specific test for dyslexia." So, what do you do? If there is not a specific test, then what? You find what works for you. This is not an easy task, and there will be struggles along the way in finding what works for you, but I have been down this road before. I have some resources to help you find what works. So, let's talk about the tips, tricks, and lessons that changed my life.

The first lesson is to get diagnosed! This might sound like the easiest step, but my entire life, I was ashamed because I knew I was different. I couldn't read as well as

---

[8]   "Dyslexia." *National Institute of Neurological Disorders and Stroke*, www.ninds.nih.gov/health-information/disorders/dyslexia?search-term=Dyslexia. Accessed 1st Jun. 2023.

[9]   "Dyslexia." *Mayo Clinic*, 6 Aug. 2022, www.mayoclinic.org/diseases-conditions/dyslexia/symptoms-causes/syc-20353552. Accessed 1st Jun. 2023.

everyone else. I couldn't understand new information at the same rate. I mentally and emotionally tortured myself because I knew I was different. A thought took over my mind—*You are a failure.* This phrase would play over and over again in my head. After years of thinking that, I'm here to tell you: It's not true. This is where the importance of getting diagnosed early comes into play. The earlier you are able to get diagnosed, the easier it is to create and develop systems to help you.

For me, waiting to get diagnosed is my one regret. If I could go back in time, I wouldn't put off my diagnosis at all. So, piece of advice number one: Get diagnosed. "Around 10% of the population has dyslexia, this can be diagnosed or undiagnosed."[10] How can we help children to get diagnosed earlier? *Dytective.* This is a software that could keep testing costs down and would allow for younger children to be diagnosed because it acts like a game.

The second piece of advice I learned is to advocate for yourself. Now, this is—by far—the hardest lesson to learn and master, but it is one that makes a difference. It took me a long time to be able to advocate for myself, but eventually, I found my own way, my own path. I used my voice, and I want to help others do the same. Advocacy is not about being forceful or expecting people to see it your way. It is about knowing what you deserve and standing up for yourself. For me, advocacy looked a lot like learning as

---

[10] Rello, L. (2016). Dytective: Diagnosing Risk of Dyslexia with a game. Retrieved February 07, 2021, from www.cs.cmu.edu/~jbigham/pubs/pdfs/2016/ PerHealth2016Dytective.pdf. Accessed 1st Jun. 2023.

much about my disability as I could and making sure that was the basis of my conversations.

I had an Individualized Education Program (IEP) in high school. This is a program that is developed to aid a student with disabilities through school and tough subjects by providing them with resources. These resources can include things like calculator use, extended time on tests and assignments, notes read aloud, and many others. These programs stick with the student into college. Each college has a program to aid its students. My program was called The Center of Disability, Access, and Resources (CDAR). This is the place where I spent a lot of time in college to make sure I passed all my exams. They provide quiet study rooms with no distractions and have special software that aids in spelling and reading answers and questions to students.

All of my accommodations from my IEP were met at CDAR. This became a resource that did its best to help me. So, find your place, whether that is a dedicated testing center or even a special room a teacher allows you to use. Whatever you do and wherever you go, as long as you know what you need to be successful, you can advocate for yourself.

The third thing to contend with is the insights you gain along the way. And this is twofold: the tips and tricks for dyslexics and the tips and tricks for the rest of the world to assist us. Right now, I have a lot of friends who are about to enter the workforce, and most of them are neurodivergent. Here are four workplace tips that are good for everyone to know, especially those who are neurodivergent. When looking into hiring a dyslexic, employers should:

1. Be flexible. Every dyslexic is special and unique when it comes to how they function with deadlines. Some dyslexics need more time to read large files, and some need auditory capabilities to understand the files. Having a manager who is willing to be flexible can help every dyslexic, since they tend to work at different paces.

2. Be understanding. It is not easy to be the dyslexic asking for help. It is not easy to ask for anything "special". When dyslexics do work up the courage to ask for help, as a manager, try to be understanding. Dyslexics are more likely to have ADD or ADHD. People with ADD, ADHD, and dyslexia are known for getting projects done because of hyperfocus and other "hidden talents", but it just may have to be on their time, so try and be understanding. These people usually put in more time and effort than most other workers, so be understanding with them when it comes to deadlines.

3. Be empathetic and sympathetic. Dyslexia is not easy to live with, and it also is not an easy thing to explain to those who do not live with dyslexia. Those who do not live with it need to understand it just as much as those who have dyslexia. Taking time to be sympathetic with these employees can help them to understand how they fit into the company. Empathic managers can also create deeper meaningful relationships with their employees.

4. Be inclusive. Although inclusivity is something that most people and companies value, it is important to note that dyslexics (and all people) want to be themselves. Most people say that they know that their organizations value inclusivity, but they are scared that their situations would fall under the label of special treatment. We need to teach all employers and employees that everyone has something that deserves to be included under the umbrella of inclusivity.

So, if that is the guidance for employers, what are the building blocks to get us to our superpowers?

Well, here are mine:

1. Use audiobooks. These are a godsend. They allow for me to get a better understanding of what I am trying to grasp when it comes to textbooks and tough subject matter.

2. Use planners. Yes, I said planners. These may not be a godsend for everyone, but they are for me. This is my way of keeping my life on track. I have a main planner and a couple other, smaller ones that have specific purposes.

3. Write with electronics. For me, it is easier to have something that has spellcheck. I also know that I stay on track and focus better on a computer than a piece of paper.

4. Glasses. Maybe this is just because I have reading glasses, but I stay on track more if I have my glasses on. This is because my eyes don't

get tired if I wear my glasses. I've just added a blue-light blocker to my glasses, but up until a few weeks ago, I had two kinds of glasses—one for computer work and one for everyday life. So, do yourself a favor and look into blue-light blockers. They help take the stress off your eyes by filtering the blue light that is emitted from our phones, TVs, and laptops. Less eye fatigue = more time to work.

5. Sticky Notes. In my opinion, you can never have enough sticky notes. I have them all over my computer and desk. Having different colored sticky notes helps because I use the different colors for different things.

6. Pens. I love a good pen. I have so many of them now that have coordinated colors that match the sticky notes and the check boxes in the planners. Everything matches, and it is because of the color-coded pens.

These are the top things that I use every day to control my Kryptonite and redefine my superpower. My things may not be the exact same things that help you, but they are a good place to start.

Society tends to classify disabilities as disadvantages, but that is not what they are—they are what make you unique. Once you know your Kryptonite, you can find your superpower. And don't forget I'm here to help you, to support you, to encourage you, and to empower you. So, join me as I continue to share my story and help you to share yours. I want to help you uncover your superpower.

All the things I have talked about with you are important, and all of them make me who I am. It has taken time, but now I see my label of dyslexia as a title I am proud of. I am so proud of who I am and the things that make me who I am—all of them. I hope you understand a little bit more about dyslexia and a little bit more about who I am, and that living life as a dyslexic doesn't have to be any different or less than. We still do all the same things that everyone else does; we just might have to rewtie—I mean rewrite—a word or sentence every once in a while.

The joys of being a Dyslexic can be few and far between when first starting out, but that is what I am here for—to be your support system, your cheerleader, your resource queen, and your guide through an experience that changes your life, in the best ways possible. Yes, dyslexia has its speed bumps, but that is not the point where you stop. That is the point where you start. So, to help you get started, I have included a *free* resource guide at the end of this book of my top five additional helpful hints to walk you through this journey of Dyslexia.

ADDITIONAL RESOURCES

"Know the Signs of Learning Disorders in Kids." *Mayo Clinic*, 18 Feb. 2023, www.mayoclinic.org/healthy-lifestyle/childrens-health/in-depth/learning-disorders/art-20046105. Accessed 1st Jun. 2023.

Nixon, Geoff. "8 Life Hacks for People with Dyslexia." *Gemm Learning*, 8 Mar. 2023, www.gemmlearning.com/blog/dyslexia/dyslexia-hacks/. Accessed 1st Jun. 2023.

"Understanding Dyslexia." *Child Mind Institute*, 6
    Dec. 2022. childmind.org/article/understanding-
    dyslexia//. Accessed 1st Jun. 2023.

FINDING YOUR "AMAZING"

By Denise Bruschi

> *"The real power behind whatever success I have now was something I found within myself—something that is in all of us, I think a little piece of God just waiting to be discovered."*[11]
>
> *– Tina Turner*

I BELIEVE THAT WE need to find that "little piece of God" in each of us to learn compassion, kindness, and love for ourselves and others.

I believe that we all have a story to tell, one that would make us proud of ourselves. When you tell your story, people who hear it can relate—and it may help them find their voice. It can help you to understand yourself, and in

---

[11] Turner, Tina. "Quotation #33479 from Laura Moncur's Motivational Quotations." Quotations Page. O Magazine, December 1, 2003. http://www.quotationspage.com/quote/33479.html#:~:text=The%20real%20power%20behind%20whatever%20success%20I%20have,piece%20of%20God%20just%20waiting%20to%20be%20discovered.

my case, it has been very cathartic to learn compassion for myself while forgiving myself and others.

I believe that we all have been put on this earth to be amazing and to have awesome adventures. They could be positive or negative, quiet or crazy, but if you choose to consider them amazing, your perception will follow.

This is my story:

It was a beautiful Colorado day, full of blue skies and sunshine. Lorena and I were meeting for coffee. I had met Lorena at a meeting for women. She has written books, encourages women to know their finances, and is a public speaker. She is an amazing woman who saw potential in me—potential that I never saw.

The coffee shop we were meeting at was very bright, yet homey—someplace I felt comfortable in. We were both dressed casually, a leisurely day, the way two good friends having coffee would dress. I was reminiscing about the first time we had met for coffee. At the time, Lorena had asked me what I did for a living. I said I was a bum because I have been on worker's compensation for over 15 years due to a physical disability. Why did I say that? Because I believed I was not enough, especially when having coffee with someone so accomplished. As we were talking, I started telling her how I became disabled.

In January of 1993, I was working as a stocker at the commissary, assigned to aisle one, where the condiments were. While the cases were not large or heavy, there were a lot of different products to know. The pallet was in the middle of the aisle—it was getting to the end of my shift, and the pallet was almost empty. I was carrying a small case of condiments when I walked on the brown pallet, caught my foot in it, twisted, turned, and sat abruptly.

Ouch! The pain was shooting in my back and down my legs.

When I got up, my body was completely distorted. The top part of my torso was off to the right, and my hips were off to the left side. It was quite noticeable. My acute pain, and the disorientation of my body, was a little frightening to me and others, so they sent me home.

The next day, I went to an Army doctor, since I was a dependent at the time.

Being a dependent in the military was much like the saying, "If the army wanted you to have a wife, they would have issued you one." You used military hospitals and doctors because all you needed (at that time) was a military ID, and they would take care of you. But you also knew that the soldiers came first, and in many cases, they should. At the same time, the doctors could not be sued, so many were not held to the same standards as civilian doctors.

The doctor told me that all I needed was my back cracked. As I was lying down on the examination table, he proceeded to put my legs in a pretzel shape, turned me on my side, and cracked my back. I heard a cracking sound, so I laid there for a while, making sure I did not have any pain or weakness. But by the time I got home, I could not walk, sit, or even lie down without extreme pain. It was so excruciating that I had to crawl to the bathroom. I slept on the sofa so as not to face the stairs. I had to be cautious about turning on my side, and it was hard to find a position with no pain. Even with the huge amount of care I took when moving, I hurt.

The next morning, I called for an appointment with the original doctor, but I was told I would have to wait a week to get in. When I finally got there, I explained the symptoms to the doctor, and he said it was all in my head. Unfortunately, the doctor's statement gave my husband an excuse to agree with him.

I felt like no one was listening, that I was all alone— even my husband was completely dismissing me and my symptoms. Then I started second-guessing myself—was it all in my head?

The doctor agreed to give me a referral to a physical therapist. I called as soon as I got home but could not get an appointment for 10 days. When I finally got to physical therapy, the pain was mostly in my left leg and foot, and my toes were like jelly. I could not move them, and when someone else would move them, they had no resistance. My physical therapist told me to go to the emergency room and only speak to a neurologist. At this time, the pain was coming and going.

So, we went to the emergency room. I stated that I only wanted to speak to a neurologist, and the ER complied. When the doctor came in, he had me do some neurological tests. The doctor said that I did need surgery, but there was a six-month waiting list, as active military came first. I told him that, as long as I knew there was an end in sight, I would handle it. He asked for the CT scans that the original doctor took, so we got the scans to the doctor on Friday. On Monday, they called and said that I needed surgery right away, and they had it set up for the very next day. As it turned out, when the original doctor cracked my back, he had broken a disc in my back, and a sizeable piece was lying on the sciatic nerve in my left leg. That's why the pain had been subsiding—the nerve was dying.

After surgery, the doctor was stunned at how I managed the pain. When he walked into the room, there was a sense of seriousness and sorrow when he stated that he could not imagine the excruciating pain I was in and showed me the piece of the disk they had removed. It was about two centimeters. He stated that grown men, even soldiers, would have been in tears.

Hearing the doctor say that, I had so many feelings. Anger because I felt no one heard me or supported me. Vindication because it was not in my head. And at one point, I considered saying to my husband, "See? I was not lying."

I would need another surgery because there was so much calcium built up on my spine, and while they got off as much as they could, they could only do so much at once.

In July of 1994, I had my second back surgery, and the doctors accidentally punctured my spinal cord, which then leaked spinal fluid. To eliminate any complications, I had to be in the hospital and bedridden for a week. I laid flat on my back and was not allowed to even lift my head! When the week was over, I was allowed to get up and move around. They finally let me go home a few days after being able to get up.

In those two years of excruciating health problems, I realized that my husband had never really supported me. Support is not support if it is at the other person's convenience. So, we separated in 1995, and I moved to Colorado.

In the coming couple of years, I got a job as a paralegal—no more stocking for me. But by 1998, I was getting some weird symptoms. It felt like electric shocks with tingling and numbing sensations in my left leg. Sometimes, when I was sleeping, I would wake up with the feeling of bugs on my legs. It was so weird that I was embarrassed to tell the doctor for fear of finding out I was crazy.

But in 2000, I was diagnosed with adhesive arachnoiditis. This was due to the puncture of the spinal cord in the second surgery. My symptoms were 1) shooting pain similar to the sensation of electric shock, 2) tingling, numbness, or weakness in my legs, 3) sensations that feel like insects crawling on your skin (formication), 4) difficulty sitting for long periods of time, 5) muscle cramps and spasms in my left leg, and 6) neurogenic bladder.

Adhesive arachnoiditis is an incurable disease, "a debilitating condition characterized by persistent arachnoid inflammation leading to intrathecal scars and Dural adhesions."[12]

I remember looking up support groups for arachnoiditis. The groups (in my opinion) created more panic and negativity surrounding the disease, so I did not stay with them. On top of it all, it was hard to find a doctor who knew about arachnoiditis.

My days were filled with research, and with the research came fear and dread. Knowing that I could be paralyzed and in excruciating pain was not what I had in mind for my life. I have always been a woman who was strong and independent. My biggest fear was that I would have to be dependent on someone—my kids. Which, in

---

[12] Muacevic, Alexander, and John R. Adler. "Spinal Adhesive Arachnoiditis: A Literature Review." National Library of Medicine. National Library of Medicine: National Center for Biotechnology Information, January 12, 2023. https://doi.org/10.7759/cureus.33697.

my head, was the worst. While my adult kids were my support system, I did not want to be totally dependent on them.

By 2007, I had my third surgery, and the doctors were giving me steroid injections in my spine for pain. Since I could only get this shot every three months, the pain relief was minimal. The doctor also put me on Vicodin for pain, but even with the Vicodin, it was still there. The symptoms were getting worse, and the doctor just kept telling me to take more Vicodin—which led to an addiction. Having arachnoiditis, being addicted and having pain, plus the reclusiveness led me into a depression that was on and off for years.

While all of this was going on, I realized that I had to make a decision. I started telling myself that this was not the way I wanted to live or die. So, I got off the Vicodin— cold turkey. I just stopped taking it. It wasn't taking the pain away, and I knew I would have to deal with withdrawals— which I did—but my fear of being close to bedridden overrode the fear of pain or withdrawals. At my request, the doctor sent me to physical therapy, and I changed a lot of my diet to not include chemicals as much as I could. I stopped steroid shots, as I found out that they could make the arachnoiditis worse.

But by 2010, the doctor suggested surgery again. He showed me what was going on, and I went under the knife again. However, in my mind, I decided this would be the last time. I would do what I needed to do to be healthier.

With the physical therapy and getting out more, as well as staying away from chemicals as much as possible, I found myself getting better and better. I started doing more activities and even began outdoor recreation.

In 2021 (at 68 years old and with the help of my son), I summited Handies Peak—14,048 feet! We had to stop a lot along the way, but I made it.

I posted my summit on Facebook. My son commented, "Your tenacity, mental fortitude, and grit are traits that have always inspired me...". To hear this from my son made me realize that everything I say, how I say it, and what I do has a huge impact on my children, even as they get older. It is so positive and uplifting for me to know that my kids have seen what you can do with "tenacity, mental fortitude, and grit".

To this day, I still have nerve damage in my left leg, have left foot drop, and only two of my toes work. And for no apparent reason, there are times when my legs really ache. With the foot drop, I have to be careful of not tripping and falling. I try to walk three to four times a week, one to three miles. And I still do exercises for my back, leg, and core. I have to be careful to not stand or sit too much—even making dinner for the family can make my back and left leg hurt. When I know I will be doing a lot, I make sure the next few days are free for me to literally do nothing but lie down and take care of myself.

You may be wondering why I call this story amazing. With all I went through, I believe that it is amazing because I not only survived it, but I conquered it. I can look back on it and know that if I put my mind to anything, it will work out.

An amazing story is any story that makes you feel great, makes you smile, makes you feel like you are on top of the world—something negative or positive, quiet or crazy. It is what you want it to be. It will always make you feel good, let you know you are here for a reason, and may even help you find your purpose in life.

You may think you don't have a story. You do, but if you disagree, then my suggestion is to read stories from others. You may find something similar to your life.

So, what is your amazing story?

Here are some other ways to find your "amazing".

Find a sentence that makes you feel good and say it out loud. I say "I'm amazing" when I feel down or someone says something negative to me. There are plenty of other words if amazing is not for you. Fabulous, awesome, astounding, stunning, stupendous, wonderful—what is your word?

Hang out with people who are your people, who find you amazing (or whatever word you choose).

Listen to your most uplifting song—mine is "Unstoppable" by Sia.

Mantras are also good for building new neural pathways. For example: I love, forgive, and accept myself.

At the end of the day, when you can find love, compassion, and forgiveness for yourself and others, you can then feel how amazing you are. With that knowledge comes disrupting the innate power of putting everyone else first, giving you the power to choose to make better decisions for you and everyone around you.

FROM FEAR TO CLARITY: EMPOWERED BY A SIX-LETTER WORD: REDISCOVERING PASSION AND PURPOSE IN THE MIDST OF MY CANCER JOURNEY

By Patricia Dieudonne

"PATRICIA, WE HAVE a problem," the Doctor said. The words that followed carried a heavy weight: "The cancer—it's back!"

My mind raced and panic surged through my body, urging me to escape the chilly hospital room. But I couldn't move—I was still hooked up to tubes and cameras. The nurses attending to me wore expressions of pity and sadness, avoiding eye contact as if they didn't know what to say. The room grew silent, so silent you could almost hear a pin drop. Yet, amidst the quietness, a tiny voice in my head whispered, "You will be okay."

While I struggled to put on my clothes, the colorectal surgeon immediately began discussing treatments—chemo, radiation, and urgent surgeries that needed to be scheduled right away. He emphasized the limited time and urged me to consider my young children. My mind went blank. Consider them? They were all I could think of! How would I explain this to them, especially since they were only five and six years old? Would they understand? Would they be scared their mommy might die?

With tears streaming down my cheeks, I quickly walked out of the examination room, desperately uttering to my surgeon: "Find another way". I frantically searched for my car, lost in the parking lot. With my mind clouded by the fear and overwhelming information, I completely forgot where I had parked. I was so distraught that I couldn't even bring myself to drive. This day that was supposed to be a happy "You are Cancer Free" day had turned into a new nightmare. I sobbed uncontrollably, dialing my husband's number. The only words I managed to say were, "It's back."

The long pause on the other end of the line was confirmation of a mutual realization of fear. When I arrived home, still teary-eyed, but trying to stay strong for my children, I embraced them tightly and immediately rushed to the kitchen and the refrigerator.

I blamed the food at that moment. The doctors only deemed it bad luck, and without family history, I didn't know where else to look for answers. So, I blamed the food. I felt desperate and out of control. In a frenzy, I discarded any foods that had ingredients I could not decipher. The next stop was Whole Foods to get fresh fruits and veggies and start juicing—I decided to clean up this "mess" once and for all. Luckily, we live in the digital age, and I knew there must be at least one person that had conquered this battle before me.

After searching endless websites and articles, I found there was not only one but many from all walks of life, backgrounds, and types of cancers. I chose to follow the one that made sense for me, since his story was similar. The plan I decided to follow was by a guy named Chris Wark, who wrote a book called *Chris Beat Cancer*. A fellow cancer survivor and advocate, he became my inspiration and role model. I followed his every step, with a few modifications due to some food intolerances.

My day started with juicing, then salads and smoothies. I lived a plant-based lifestyle and took supplements to strengthen my body, but that was only the beginning. In my quest for healing, another pivotal figure emerged— my friend, Christiane Santana, a board-licensed acupuncturist. Her profound knowledge of oriental medicine opened my eyes to a whole new perspective on how the human body operates. She began to treat me and educate me about holistic principles and practices. Her compassionate guidance and therapeutic interventions played a vital role in my new journey.

After a few months, I started feeling better physically, but that lingering fear still persisted. It was during this time I noticed a recurring theme and key point among cancer survivors—the emphasis and significance to maintain a positive mindset. While it sounds easy, when you are in the midst of a challenge, acting on it feels more clouded and uncertain.

Let's take a step backward. In my twenties, I was introduced to the world of network marketing. Although I am no longer involved, that experience served as a gateway to personal development. Throughout my life, the concept of personal development and mindset reprogramming had never been addressed. Even throughout my college years, none of my professors ever touched on the importance of cultivating a positive mindset. I truly believe that pre-existing personal development journey equipped me with the tools and mindset needed to confront this dreaded six-letter-word from a fresh perspective. My main driving belief was that if one person could overcome it, so could I.

Embarking on a hermitting quest to decipher and learn about what causes cancer and why I was the only person in my family with this disease led me on a beautiful journey of transformation. I delved into the depths of what I consider the three pillars of holistic healing and fortification. These three pillars, which intertwine harmoniously, offer guidance in navigating life's challenges. Body synergy, spirituality, prayer and positive mindset psychology formed the basis of my journey.

My mission for this challenge became clear: Work through emotions and any trauma, eat clean, cut out any processed foods, and strengthen my body so I could go through radiation and surgery with a strong and positive mindset.

After developing a structured daily food schedule and practicing meal prepping, nourishing my body became a seamless endeavor. However, it was in the spiritual realm that I encountered unexpected revelations. As a Catholic, my connection with God deepened even further through prayer as a daily practice. Yet, buried traumas and forgiveness tested my resilience in a capacity for healing. During my healing, I enlisted various mentors such as energy healers, life coaches, and cancer coaches to help me. This choice led me to recognize trauma from childhood, which was ingrained.

When I was growing up, terms such as "gaslighting" and "narcissism" were unheard of. The idea that actual family members had committed these acts against and around me was also unthought of. My beliefs about myself were formed by the statements of others.

"She always cries in pictures."

"Oh, she is shy."

"She is not that good in math."

"She is always scared."

These statements became my personality, and that's just how I was. Hiding inside my shell and not speaking up was just what I did. Getting coaching really helped me understand I was holding onto grief, anger, frustration, and so many other emotions because of ideas that "labeled" me but were not mine. Now, as for the work of shedding those ideas and actually figuring out who I was—let me tell you, it was not easy. Forgiving those family members was even harder, but having coaches helped me eliminate those deep, ingrained past traumas and led me to an inner transformation. Soon, I realized the true catalyst for change was within me—my own mindset. My trusted friend.

Mindset is not only limited to approaching cancer. It is pivotal for pursuing entrepreneurship or chasing after that promotion—and even cultivating unwavering self-esteem. Positive mindset also propelled me toward achieving multiple six figures while I was working in my real estate career, even when the path appeared uncertain, at times. It became the compass guiding me through the darkest corners of fear, igniting a flicker of hope when it seemed all was lost. My daily positive mindset practice helped me transition from the realm of fear to one of conquering, hope, and joy.

After the storm, came the calm. With the guidance of a dedicated team of doctors, I went through multiple surgeries and underwent intense short-term radiation treatments to eliminate the cancer from my body. During the recovery phase, it became clear that I no longer desired to return to the stress and demands of my successful real estate career. Thus, the search for my true purpose became my primary focus. Where could I create an impact? How could I touch others' lives to strengthen their beliefs and families?

Leveraging my background in business, as well as my bachelor's degree in psychology, I embarked on a quest to pursue various coaching certifications to deepen my understanding of how to guide others through their challenges and bridge the gap for my future clients. As a mother, my attention gravitated toward supporting fellow moms who grapple with the challenges of balancing their roles as caregivers while pursuing successful careers or businesses—also known as "Mom Guilt". Their struggles resonated deeply with me, igniting a commitment to provide guidance, encouragement, and practical solutions tailored to their unique challenges.

You don't need to undergo a big, dramatic, life-changing experience like mine to go through transformation. Transformation can happen, with determination, in any aspect of life. The three pillars I mentioned earlier are incorporated in my signature coaching method and are versatile enough to be applied to any situation. Here are a few practical ways for you to apply them and empower yourself when you are going through challenges:

The first pillar is body synergy, which is a two-part system. The first is prioritizing a healthy lifestyle, which includes nourishing your body with wholesome foods. The foods we consume play a vital role in nourishing the body. It is crucial to be mindful of our intake of processed foods, and whenever possible, prioritize fresh meals made of whole ingredients. The nourishment we provide to our body directly impacts its optimal functioning. When we consume excessive artificial colors, sugars, and other additives, our bodies can become lethargic and sluggish. By embracing a wholesome, natural approach to nutrition, we can fuel our bodies for vitality and sustained wellbeing.

The second part of body synergy is movement. It helps not only to enhance energy levels but also boosts self-esteem. Stepping outside and basking in the sunlight goes beyond simply absorbing essential vitamins; it is grounding and promotes the regulation of the nervous system. This, in turn, leads to improved sleep quality, reduced anxiety, and diminished feelings of panic. Carving out a minimum of 10 minutes each day to venture outdoors, inhaling the fresh air, and embracing the gratitude of breathing deeply into your lungs becomes a transformative practice in nurturing the body. Engaging in various forms of exercise, be it a brisk walk, jog, or even the serene movement of yoga or Tai Chi allows you to embrace the beauty of movement and strengthen your physical wellbeing.

The second pillar is spirituality. I strongly believe that cultivating a strong connection with God, or any other higher power that resonates with you, is crucial for healing. When we have faith in a higher power, we can release our problems and surrender them to the universe, relieving ourselves of the burden. Prayer plays a significant role in my daily routine, and I include a brief prayer each morning to seek guidance and solace.

Another form of spirituality is meditation. It allows me to find inner calmness and silence the negative thoughts that often clutter my mind. By clearing our minds through meditation, we can maintain a positive outlook and cultivate a sense of peace within ourselves. As opposed to popular belief, meditation does not have to be a long practice to be effective. Just a few minutes per day will help establish a daily habit of self-care and self-discovery. Consider integrating some form of spiritual practice in your daily morning routine. Dedicate just five to 10 minutes to your personal wellbeing, and notice the positive changes as they start occurring.

The third pillar is positive mindset psychology. Reprogramming our subconscious and shifting from a negative to a positive mindset takes time and effort. It is definitely not a "one hit wonder". When we are faced with challenges, it's the fear of the unknown that holds us back, leaving us feeling stuck and unsure. We feel paralyzed because of the uncertainty.

There are powerful tools we can use to overcome these barriers. Affirmations, visualization, and journaling are just a few techniques I, personally, employ to reprogram my mindset. At first, it might feel foreign, but when practiced consistently, the results are astounding. These practices help silence the negative inner dialogue, allowing space to release overthinking and for positivity and clarity to flourish. Remember, there are various approaches to developing a positive mindset, so find what resonates with you and make it a daily habit. Only when it becomes second nature will you witness its transformative power in action.

It is my sincere hope that this transformative journey has served as an inspiration and touched your heart, encouraging you to face your own challenges with a renewed perspective. Just as David had unwavering faith when facing Goliath, may you find the strength within yourself to embark on your own transformational path. Embrace the belief that you, too, have the power to transform your life and overcome any obstacles that come your way.

CHOOSING TO THRIVE

By Karleen Wagner

IT WAS 2011, and I had just turned 40. I was fully enjoying life with my husband and our two boys. I had found my passion in empowering and training adults and children in martial arts and had recently received my third-degree black belt. I was plugging along until the day I got "the call". Have you ever received "the call"? That one phone call that causes life from that moment forward to shift and change? For me, that call was from my doctor. I had not been feeling well for over two years, and my previous doctor had told me I was just getting older and that our bodies don't work as well as we age. Well... that is a true statement, but I was only 40!

It got to the point where my neighbors began wondering why I was "hiding out" and not socializing. I started looking up my symptoms on Google (yes, we all do it) and thought I might have thyroid issues. It made sense; my dad also had thyroid issues, which can be hereditary. Armed with this bit of information, I made a call to my gynecologist and requested to have bloodwork done. Based on my symptoms, he agreed it might be my thyroid. Boy, were we both wrong!

Back to the day I received "the call". It was my doctor on the other line, and he began by saying, "I have good news, and I have bad news."

I'm not sure that is ever the best way to start a conversation, but I went along and said, "Tell me the good news."

The good news was my thyroid was just fine. I shifted in my seat a little bit and then asked, "Okay... then what is the bad news?"

He had run a full bloodwork panel, including blood cell counts and organ functions, specifically kidney and liver. Unbeknownst to either of us, I was in kidney failure. At the time of the test, I was at 22% function and dropping.

Kidney what? I've never had anything wrong with my kidneys! How is this happening? Why is this happening? What do we do now? I had all the questions and then some. First things first, we needed to find out why my kidneys were failing and what my treatment options were. I was referred to another doctor, who did various tests to determine why an otherwise perfectly healthy 40-year-old would go into kidney failure. The results came back, and they were quite shocking. I am the proud recipient of a genetic disease called Polycystic Kidney Disease. But wait... there's more! No one in my family has this dominant gene, so in addition to having it, I'm a mutation!

Well, now we knew what we were dealing with, and I could put a name to that ugly and life-changing diagnosis. Here is what I found out: There is no treatment, no cure, and no recovery for my condition. My options were limited, and none of them were part of my life plan. In the long run, I would need a kidney transplant, which had a three- to five-year waitlist. For now, I would be preparing to go on dialysis so we would be ready when my kidneys could no longer filter my blood effectively. At the time, it felt like life as I knew it would be over. How could I possibly continue my current lifestyle while experiencing kidney failure and having to go on dialysis? What kind of mom would I be? What kind of wife would I be? How was I going to continue to create income?

Let's take a break here and talk about what happens when an event like this upends your life. I'm sure you've experienced something that has just rocked your world. One day, things are status quo, and the next, you're dealing with a situation you had not prepared for. Maybe it's a divorce, the loss of a loved one, a medical diagnosis, the loss of a job, or something else. Fill in the blank for yourself. How do you respond when this happens? At the time, it's okay to be sad, angry, and frustrated. You need to take time to feel the hurt and the pain; we need to grieve. However, this isn't a place to get stuck in. Sooner or later, it is time to make a plan, put the past behind, and look toward the future. How your future plays out is connected to the choices you make now.

I want you to hear this... you do have a choice. You can wallow in what has just happened, remove yourself from life and all that was previously "normal", or you can choose to overcome. Life happens to all of us; no single person will go through it unscathed. You can either accept this reality or live in fear of what is next. Are you able to find the blessing in the midst of tragedy? Are you listening for the soft whisper of hope or only acknowledging the challenges yelling at you?

Hear this as well... you don't need to do it alone! If you are open to it, so many resources are available to you when you are ready to move forward. For me, my friends and family were an incredible source of support and encouragement. At that moment, however, I knew that changes needed to be made to design the life I desired.

At the time of my diagnosis, I was training in martial arts five times a week, sometimes twice a day. I was running the academy my family and I trained at, as well as a program through our local recreation center. I was teaching and training nearly every day. Suddenly, I was looking at possible dialysis, which would definitely limit my ability to train and continue at that pace. My transplant coordinators suggested I begin looking for a living kidney donor.

Finding a living donor before I had to go on dialysis was the ideal scenario to maintain my health. Talk about a humbling experience, asking another person to voluntarily go under the knife to give me one of their organs. My boys were nine and 11 at the time, and my desire to be completely present for them outweighed my fear and my pride when it came to asking someone to donate a kidney to me. So, I put the word out. I was, again, humbled when I had ten people offer to get tested. The first to get tested was a young woman I had been developing a relationship with over the previous few years. She was approved as a match, and in under a year, I received the gift of life without having to go on dialysis.

By the time I received my transplant, I was down to about 8% kidney function, so I received this blessing just in time. As of this writing, it has been 11 years, and her kidney has made itself at home in my body. Aside from some crummy medications I have to take (and their side effects), my quality of life is considerably better than I expected it to be. Still, changes needed to be made. This kidney is a gift I am not willing to take for granted, so I hit the internet. This time, I went down the rabbit hole of how amazing our organs of elimination (kidneys and liver) are and how much we abuse them.

Our body has the incredible ability to keep us in homeostasis. Still, over time, our organs and systems can wear down if we don't care for ourselves. I began to learn about toxins in our food and the products we use every day. Preservatives, chemicals, artificial colors, and flavorings are just a sampling of what we expose our bodies to daily—from processed food to household cleaners and personal care products.

I started reading labels and identifying ingredients in the personal care products I used. I also took a look at our household cleaners: detergents, window cleaners, bathroom and kitchen cleaners. I was absolutely shocked at how many chemicals I was exposing myself and my family to every single day. I made the choice to begin purchasing organic, local, and farm-fresh foods, limiting my intake of processed foods and fast foods. In the search for companies that provided toxin-free products, I stumbled upon the next chapter of my life.

I chose to partner with a company that produces clean personal care and nutritional supplements and found other companies to use that provided clean home care products. I was on a mission to share and educate others about what I had learned. Often times, we don't really consider our health until a health crisis brings it front and center. By that time, it may be too late. I wanted to reach people before they were forced to make a change, while it was still a choice.

I have always enjoyed speaking, teaching, and empowering others but never felt I had a platform to do it on my own. I was raised on the importance of having a job to provide for yourself and your family. The thought of being an entrepreneur was scary, and yet, exciting.

After my transplant, I needed to slow down my training to protect my new kidney, and I found I was no longer satisfied working for someone else and working set hours. I desired more flexibility and wanted to make a bigger impact. I slowly began to set out on my own to help others create both health and wealth. My definition of health includes physical, mental, and emotional health. My company, Choosing to Thrive, is the result of making the choice to overcome what life handed me and choosing to thrive rather than just survive.

I would not wish for anyone to have organ failure and go through a transplant and everything beyond. However, if it were not for this event in my life, I'm not sure I would have had the inspiration to set out on my own. It did not come easily, and it did not happen instantaneously—in fact, I am still defining myself and my business, and it is constantly evolving.

Are you living a life of survival, or are you thriving? Take a quick inventory of where you are at.

What does it look like to survive:

- living in stress
- being reactive
- living for the second, the minute, the hour, or the day and never looking toward the future
- living in the past
- no longer dreaming

- negative outlook, blaming others
- inward focus (focusing on yourself or your own needs)
- decisions are made based on your current circumstances
- rigidity, feeling stuck
- decreased mental and physical health
- increase in bad habits (such as increased alcohol consumption, poor eating, lack of exercise)
- decreased pleasure in life and the things you do
- just going through the motions
- What does it look like to thrive:
- living in hope
- being proactive
- setting goals, planning for the future
- taking responsibility
- positive outlook
- outward (others) focused
- decisions are made on possibility, looking at what the future holds
- flexibility and moving forward
- feelings of joy
- increased mental and physical health
- you see the future for what it can create and what you can create
- the world is at your fingertips

Where are you right now? Is that where you want to be? I want to leave you with some action steps to move yourself from merely surviving to truly thriving in your own life.

First, I believe developing a habit of gratitude can benefit you in more ways than one. It can help improve your outlook on the world and toward others, it can change your mindset and how you proceed with your day, and it can bring you from a place of worry and discouragement to a place of hope and possibility.

I bookend my days with gratitude. When I wake up in the morning, before I even open my eyes, I think of three things I am grateful for. At night, when the light goes out, I do the same. By starting the day with gratitude, I am setting myself up for success; I choose to begin my day by looking at what is good in my life. At night, I repeat the process so that as I fall asleep, I'm again in the space of thankfulness instead of thinking about all the would-have-beens or could-have-beens. Take a small step right now and think of three things you are grateful for, then repeat this process daily.

Second, how are you nurturing your mind? Are you consuming the local news, social media, video games, and reality shows? Do you surround yourself with positive and uplifting people or those who are complaining and in survival mode themselves? The environments we choose to expose ourselves to greatly impact our mental and emotional health. If you don't have a great work environment, consider making the bold move to a new job. Maybe your personal life is challenging. You may need to reevaluate who you choose to spend time with. You have the choice in how and where you spend your time. It may not be easy to make a change, and it may take time, but you have the power to create the future you desire.

Third, I believe that self-care is a success strategy! What are you doing to take care of your body? Are you taking time to relax and decrease your stress? Are you fueling your body with healthy foods and drinks? Do you take time during your day to get up and move? Take the time right now and choose one thing that relaxes you— that you also enjoy doing. Maybe curling up with a good book, taking your dog for a walk, listening to soothing music, or taking a steamy bubble bath appeals to you. Find something that allows your mind and body to quiet down, and then make it a priority to do that daily. It can take as little as 15 minutes or last longer, if you can manage it. Amid the hustle, take time to care for yourself!

Creating new habits doesn't happen by accident. I am intentional about adding these activities to my day. I make time because I know that, by doing so, I am bringing my best into the world. When I take time to focus on self-care, I become more productive in my day, as well. Are you ready to choose a healthier lifestyle for yourself?

My diagnosis and subsequent transplant could have allowed me to spiral into the abyss. Life as I knew it would change, and I had a choice to make: Do I hold on with both hands to reclaim the life I had, or do I create a more vibrant future? The past is comfortable, and I know many people who like to live there. However, when you live in the past, you forfeit your future. Are you satisfied with merely surviving... or are you ready to *thrive*?

CONCLUSION

*A*S THE STORIES presented here have showcased, regardless of who you are, life is usually filled with many bumps in the road. Add entrepreneurship, and the whole journey becomes one not suited for the faint of heart. I shared earlier how I faced resistance from family and my own personal fears about my business. Along the rocky road, however, I birthed my very own personal growth framework for women entrepreneurs that eventually transformed into a best-selling, award winning book and a TEDx talk.

Now, by using the five steps of **The Empowered Woman's Path** framework and compiling the experiences shared on these pages, my hope is that you have discovered you are not alone on your path toward self-empowerment. You now have 21 examples to draw inspiration from and 21 real people you can connect with using the information in the About the Authors section to start an empowerment movement.

With **Notice Yourself**, Janae, Randi, Anna, and Terri emphasized that self-empowerment begins with recognizing your true essence and uniqueness, paving the way to authenticity and individuality.

In **Listen to Yourself**, Deanna, Krista, Marti, and Marit shed light on the importance of listening to our inner dialogue and spoken words. This is how we face self-sabotage head-on and uncover personal barriers that hinder achievement and fulfillment.

Through **Forgive Yourself**, Barbara, Bella, Paris, Monika, and Vesta highlighted a pivotal stage in this self-empowerment journey, where they have taken the time to embrace their imperfections in order to transform failure, guilt, and shame into invaluable life lessons.

In **Empower Yourself**, Nina, Lorena, Pamela, and Neha brought insight into the benefits of celebrating our strengths and flaws to reclaim our personal power by taking responsibility for our own happiness and achievements.

Finally, **Transform Yourself** showcased how our personal transformation carries impactful ripples into our surroundings, as illustrated by Delaney, Denise, Patricia, and Karleen.

As you strengthen your belief in yourself enough to show yourself grace and shamelessly enjoy all that you are, may your transformational journey be just the beginning of an empowerment domino effect.

Join me in creating a culture that celebrates accomplishments, honors unwavering determination, and unlocks untapped potential in ourselves, past generations, and generations to come.

Be empowered!

ABOUT THE AUTHORS

MARTA SPIRK

EMPOWERMENT COACH & VISIBILITY STRATEGIST

ORN AND raised in Brazil, and after building a career of 20 years in communication, specializing in teaching foreign languages, translating, and interpreting, Marta got married and moved to the United States. With the surprise of a triplet pregnancy, at nine months post-partum in late 2016, she felt pulled to start her own coaching business to help women move past perfectionism, impostor syndrome, and comparison and into visibility, credibility, and profit.

Through the years, she's supported thousands of women entrepreneurs to use their voices, taking her business to multiple six figures in sales, publishing her first book *The Empowered Woman: The Ultimate Roadmap to Business Success* and speaking on TEDx. Marta has also added music to her repertoire, releasing her first single, "Show Yourself".

It is her passion and mission to be a role model for women, exemplifying that everything is impossible until you do it. Her goal is to give women both the permission to succeed and a platform to let their voices be heard.

Has this book encouraged you in your personal and entrepreneurial journey? Marta would love to hear from you. Share how the book has made a difference in your life by writing to contact@martaspirk.com.

If you're ready for more inspiration and ideas, you can find them on Marta's podcast, *The Empowered Woman*, anywhere you listen to podcasts: www.martaspirk.com/podcast.

Marta has also created a unique program called *The Empowered Woman School*. This is a membership intended to enhance personal and business growth for women entrepreneurs. It is designed to give you content, coaching, and community as a form of accountability in the implementation of The Empowered Woman's Path and to provide specific strategies to grow your business. As a reader of this book, you are now a part of the Empowered Woman family and eligible to claim a 30-day free trial to the school. Go to www.freegiftfrommarta.com to get started.

Finally, you can book Marta as a professional speaker for your next event. She is an international speaker who has appeared on KWGN-TV and KDVR/FOX31 Denver as well as TEDx and on worldwide podcasts and events. Her high energy and impactful message will inspire your audience, and she will leave them empowered to take action. Marta uses the power of stories to encourage everyone to live an empowered life by seeing challenges and adversity as lessons and stepping-stones to create their desired reality. Please contact us via email at contact@martaspirk.com.

Be empowered!

JANAE ANDRUS COX
CCM, PMP, MBA, CONNECTION EXPERT

*J*ANAE IS the creator of Touch & Tell, a card game for increasing emotional intimacy between couples. As a connection expert, Janae has worked for 15+ years in various industries to help companies streamline their processes and build their user communities more effectively by improving their professional connections. For the past six years, she has also helped couples improve their personal connections with each other through her own company, Touch & Tell.

Visit touchandtellgame.com to purchase your game today.

Free gift! Get your free digital card samples at touchandtellgame.com/empoweredwoman.

RANDI JO PIEPER

$\mathcal{R}$ AISED IN northeastern Montana, Randi Jo Pieper's roots were firmly grounded in a family of caregivers and dedicated professionals. Her upbringing, shaped by a firefighter, undercover sheriff, and farm equipment salesman father, alongside a nurturing nurse mother, instilled in her a profound sense of compassion and responsibility from an early age. As the eldest of three sisters, Randi Jo naturally assumed a "maternal role" when her mother underwent back surgery and her younger sibling was diagnosed with celiac disease at the tender age of three.

When embarking on her journey, Randi Jo started her career as a probation officer in 2004, helping men and women who filled their "voids" with addictions. Over the course of her professional career, she has helped thousands of people of all ages reintegrate into society and find their places in the world. She holds a master's degree in teaching and learning online, a bachelor's degree in criminal justice, and is an unlicensed psychotherapist. After years of working with men and women on a deeper level, she decided to become a life coach in 2013.

Recently, Randi Jo has been actively engaging with "problem solvers/caretakers" within the criminal justice field, unfolding valuable wisdom on rejuvenation and reclaiming personal fulfillment. She shares a three-step process, empowering individuals to break free from stagnant routines and rediscover the joy that once fueled their work. By embracing these steps, professionals can effectively replenish their own emotional well-being, ultimately enhancing their ability to serve and make a positive impact in their roles.

Connect with Randi Jo: www.findingyourblissllc.com

Visit her website to claim your *free* workbook titled *Empowered Within*. This comprehensive resource guides readers through introspective exercises, empowering affirmations, and practical strategies to cultivate self-love and unleash their full potential.

ANNA CHENEY

ANNA CHENEY, born an American in the country of Germany, travels abroad with her military family. She is the youngest of eight children.

She started dating her husband at the age of 15, was married by 19, and was blessed with her first child by her 21st birthday. Their family grew with two more children and the gift of three grandsons. She celebrates her life and love with her husband of 38 years.

An influencer in her community as a leader in a women's connection company, Anna is also a gifted transformational life coach who supports her clients in creating personalized lifestyles that are doable and sustainable so they can live a better life! She can enable you to identify the areas in your life where self-abandonment has overtaken your life's purpose.

Anna teaches you how to build a successful life by taking back your power and creating the necessary harmony— emotionally, physically, mentally, and spiritually—to sustain your new rhythm. She helps you learn to observe your heart's nudges as it leads you where your spirit longs to soar. Anna shares her personal experience of living through a long and stressful journey, not just surviving but thriving as she pivoted into continued success. Anna will share with you the five integral pillars that helped her soar with brave wings so she could continue to fly and achieve her dreams.

Connect with Anna: www.lifesharmonycoaching.com

Claim a *free* 60-minute discovery call by contacting her at lifesharmonycoaching@gmail.com.

TERRI MONGAIT

*T*ERRI MONGAIT is a certified Equine Gestalt Coach, Canfield Methodology Trainer, and transformational speaker. She is an award-winning author of *Finding True Purpose ~ Life Beyond the Castle*. Her expertise lies in overcoming the obstacles and unraveling the stories that keep her clients from living their best, most successful lives. She is currently writing her next book, *Unraveling Your PTS*, which will guide the reader to uncover their own Post Traumatic Stories that are keeping them from living their authentic lives. By partnering with her herd of wisdom horses at Begin Again Ranch, Terri gets to the root of what's currently holding her clients back from being their most awesome selves and teaches them the tools they need to stride with confidence into the future of the dreams they actually deserve.

She is also a respected spiritual teacher and host of the "Soul Wisdom Transitions" podcast. With deep knowledge and a compassionate approach, she offers insights and wisdom to help individuals navigate life's transitions with clarity and grace. Through her podcast, client coaching, and written work, Terri empowers listeners and clients to embrace their own soul journeys and awaken their spiritual potential. Her teachings and guidance have touched the lives of many, making her an influential voice in the realm of soul wisdom and personal growth.

Visit Terri's website at www.beginagainranch.com to read about her work or at www.soulwisdomtransitions.com to check out her podcast.

You can contact Terri at terri@beginagainranch.com to begin unraveling your own stories.

DEANNA MERLINO

$\mathcal{D}$EANNA MERLINO prides herself on being a committed wife, present momma, and multi-passioned entrepreneur offering all-encompassing healing & expansion. By trade, she is an elite personal trainer focusing as a sports nutritionist and transformation specialist, with a personal training app called DM Fit. Affectionately referred to as "The Empowered Coach", Deanna is the host of the *EmpowereD with Deanna Merlino* podcast and an intuitive life coach and quantum energetic healer helping her clients to thrive on all levels mind, body, and soul. She is the creator & CEO of The Empowered Academy, a globally recognized training provider of transformational accredited online courses and the co-founder/owner of The Empowered Collective, providing in-person spiritual retreats and an online membership/community. She wears yet another hat as a vacation rental & retreat space owner/manager.

Experience a free week of her healing membership by entering code: FREEWEEK at checkout on her website, www.theempoweredcollective.podia.com/membership.

Contact:
Email- contact@deannamerlinofit.com
Instagram handle: @theempoweredcoach333
Website: www.deannamerlino.podia.com

KRISTA GARRETT

*A*S THE daughter of an Air Force pilot that was raised by rice and cattle farmers and a homemaker mother who came from cotton farmers in Western Texas, Krista Garrett learned from an early age the importance of hard work and education while developing a deep love for music. Beginning piano lessons at the age of eight, Krista dreamed of pursuing a career as a concert pianist. As a teen, she attended a performing arts high school and determined that the coveted acceptance into conservatory was physically and mentally out of her reach. As a result, Krista pursued an undergraduate degree in psychology and a masters in developmental psychology from Johns Hopkins.

For a period of time, she worked in the field as an EEG technician and neurofeedback therapist for a thriving neurology practice. In 2006, she met the owner of a local music school while teaching a psychology course at a local college, and her passion for music was reignited.

Leaving the neurology practice, Krista joined her husband at his music school. After marrying in 2007, she and her husband had twin daughters in 2011 and a son in 2015. Her husband left the business in 2014 to pursue his degree in theology, and Krista took on the full-time responsibilities of the school.

As the present owner of the Garrett Music Academy, Krista took her passion for music and the mind and created a private music school that not only offers private music lessons for all instruments and voices, but she created a series of programs that address mental health and developmental/neurodivergent needs. The mental health program, Find Your Voice, is a marriage between journaling, lyric writing, and music composition, where coping strategies for depression and anxiety create art.

In addition to being a wife, mother and entrepreneur, Krista is currently serving as a teaching fellow with the Department of Psychology at Harvard University as well as an adjunct faculty member for Coastal Carolina University in South Carolina.

To learn more about how music can support your mental health and wellbeing, book a free one hour consultation with Krista to discuss your goals and create a plan through methods such as the Find Your Voice Program, Sound Healing or Private Lessons. To schedule, email kgarrett.garrettmusicacademy@gmail.com.

www.garrettmusicacademy.com (410) 286-5505

MARTI STATLER

M ARTI STATLER is the founder of Rebel Queen, podcast host of *The Rebel Maker*, owner of No Ice Liquid Catering, and part-time real estate investor. She spends her days creating tools and resources that support women in building a life and business they desire.

Contact:
RebelQueen.co
Facebook & Insta: @rebelqueenbooks
Email: marti@rebelqueen.co

MARIT HUDSON

*B*ORN IN Norway and raised in the UK, Marit is a qualified attorney in England and the Cayman Islands, where she works in a leading global law firm. Marit has also obtained her MBA from the University of Florida.

Marit is passionate about professional development, corporate wellness, fitness, and coaching. She holds several coaching certifications and enjoys writing content to share her coaching knowledge and experience with a wider audience.

Marit is also a proponent of supporting youth through mentorship and works with One2One in the Cayman Islands (formerly Big Brothers Big Sisters of the Cayman Islands).

Go to www.marithudson.com to download your free e-book of positive affirmations.

Connect with Marit on Instagram: @marithudson

BARBARA CONWAY

ARBARA CONWAY, a certified transformational mindset life coach, brings over three decades of mentoring experience to her transformative work. Having navigated a traumatic divorce and emerged stronger, Barbara discovered her true calling: empowering women to reclaim their identities, boost their confidence, and achieve their goals.

In her debut book chapter, Barbara shares practical insights and actionable steps for fostering a growth mindset. Her passion for personal development and ability to connect resonate through every page. Barbara's work is a testament to resilience, positivity, and the unwavering belief in one's potential. She continues to inspire women to lead confident, purposeful lives.

You can connect with Barbara at BarbaraConway.com or email her at Barbara@BarbaraConway.com.

Please feel free to accept this gift of her eBook, *101 Ways to Motivate Yourself for Success*–https://bit. ly/101WaystoMotivate

BELLA BLISS

*B*ELLA BLISS is an intuitive "Transformational and Empowerment Life Coach", international bestselling author, visionary leader, inspirational speaker, and InnerBLISS Alchemist.

Bella specializes in elevating soulpreneurs—empowering motivated women to radiate energy inward and inviting them to play in the quantum playground of limitless possibility—so that her clients can unleash their soul-fire and fiercely live their passionate truth as the InnerBLISS Goddess they already are.

Bella offers a wide range of transformative coaching programs and retreats that are based on "the soul only knows love." Her clients will learn how to embrace mystery and enjoy the ride as they face the darkness in life with courage, take inspired action, and celebrate the deliciousness of her InnerBLISS Goddess life every day.

The empowering mantra she teaches and lives by is: "Be SEEN. Be HEARD. Be LIMITLESS."

You can connect with Bella on all social media platforms and sign up for her email list with exciting updates here: www.innerblissgoddess.com.

Take control of your life and tap into your inner guidance system. Be sure to download the free InnerBLISS GPS guide today! InnerBLISS GPS is a guide that helps women to navigate life's challenges by providing tools and techniques to tap into inner wisdom and intuition. It teaches how to cultivate awareness and mindfulness, overcome limiting beliefs, and develop intuition and inner wisdom. The guide is easy to follow and implement, with step-by-step instructions and exercises, providing a deeper understanding of one's unique path in life.

PARIS BYRUM

*A*S A single, homeschooling mama of six children, a lover of Jesus, and a creative soul, Paris weaves her personal journey into a tapestry of inspiration committed to stirring others to love and commit good works.

With Hello Productive Mama, a lifestyle management business, a background in wedding and event coordination, and a passion for helping women achieve productivity and time sustainability, her wisdom and guidance will uplift and transform your life.

Join her at www.helloproductivemama.com/balancingbrilliance, where she helps working mamas balance their brilliance in the midst of suffering and chaos.

MONIKA NIELSEN

*A*S A self-proclaimed first generation purger, Monika Nielsen understands the emotional ties we all have to the clothing in our wardrobe, along with the frustration and emotional toll it can take when we get ready amidst the chaos of an overflowing closet.

Monika's expertise extends far beyond just organizing your closet: She helps her clients untangle the deeply rooted stories behind clothing and self-worth. Stop thinking it'll be someday when you have another life or another body... you are worthy of feeling fiercely confident and supremely beautiful—right here, right now!

Monika will empower you to drop the guilt, honor the memories, and get you sorted out and set up so you can go out and do the things you're meant to do!

Connect with Monika at www.yourstylerehabist.com and click on your free guide: 10 Questions to Ask in Your Closet or on IG @StyleClosetCoach

VESTA HAGER

$\bigvee$ESTA HAGER is an experienced motivational speaker, trainer, author, successful podcaster, and Retreat Maven. She is passionate about inspiring women to lead the life they want to live.

Her method, Dream. Decide. Do., is the framework for the new life you want to design. She offers coaching, retreats, and workshops to help every woman live her next chapter on her own terms. She believes we are all the Leading Lady in our own movie. Be the STAR you were born to be.

Connect with her here to start planning your next chapter: https://www.vestatalks.com/dream-decide-do

NINA MACARIE

*N*INA MACARIE is a visibility expert helping female entrepreneurs get more visibility and connect with dream clients through podcast interviews. She is the creator of the P.I.T.C.H. podcasts framework, helping clients pitch themselves to the right podcasts with ease and confidence in an authentic way.

After sending hundreds and hundreds of podcast pitches, and also seeing what kind of pitches are put out in the world, Nina knows exactly what elements to include in a successful pitch. Not only did she get amazing feedback from her successfully booked clients, but she also impressed the podcast hosts that she pitched to.

Today, Nina's mission is to help female online entrepreneurs, coaches, course creators, consultants, and podcasters get an amazing first impression as they start spreading their messages on other people's platforms.

Nina lives in Romania with her husband, two kids, and three cats. You can check out her website: https://oneluckystar.com or connect with her on one of the following platforms:

Instagram: https://instagram.com/nina_macarie
Facebook: https://www.facebook.com/nina.macarie.3/
LinkedIn: https://www.linkedin.com/in/nina-macarie-58953b44/

Download your roadmap to starting your speaking journey: https://oneluckystar.com/start

LORENA ARNOLD

$\mathcal{B}$ ORN AND raised in Mexico City, Lorena Arnold demonstrated her entrepreneurial spirit by moving to and thriving in the United States. She went on to get a bachelor's degree in information systems, raised two sons, and now is a proud grandmother.

She is an author, motivational speaker, woman entrepreneur, and money breakthrough business coach and founder of the Women on FIRE academy. For the past 10 years, she has worked with women entrepreneurs who want to live a joyful, abundant life but who struggle with worry and concerns (doubt and fears) about money and never having enough. She teaches new ways of creating, managing, investing, and manifesting money so that her clients can have a more empowered life.

Lorena Arnold believes in a new conversation about money, leading from scarcity to an abundant life. She believes life is an adventure and is too short to take the slow route to wealth. She believes in being on FIRE—the state of wonder and joy. Lorena understood what it meant to suddenly be faced with decisions about where to live and how to manage finances.

Her training helps and supports women spiritually and emotionally with financial insights they can use immediately to begin creating and growing their financial futures. Lorena is a certified money breakthrough business coach and Thriving Method facilitator. She speaks at conferences and companies committed to leadership and personal development and unlocking people's potential. How you "invest" yourself in time, energy, and attention determines the quality of your experience of money in your life.

Connect with Lorena at: www.LorenaArnold.com

Claim your free success guide, *Queen of Money – 15 Ways to Instantly Start Becoming the Queen of Money in Your Business*, here: https://tinyurl.com/QueenOfMoney

PAMELA MAASS GARRETT

$\mathcal{P}$AMELA MAASS Garrett is an award-winning estate planning and asset protection attorney and CEO of Law Mother LLC, a law firm she founded to help parents protect their futures and loved ones.

Pamela is the author of the bestselling book, *Legally Ever After*.

Download a free copy of *Legally Ever After* at Lawmother.com/fbook and discover the six-step plan to protect your children's future and happiness. Pamela is on a mission to simplify legal, tax, and financial strategies for parents.

Connect with Pamela on social media @LawMother.

NEHA NAIK

*N*EHA NAIK is the CEO of three businesses: a recruitment agency, a sleep consultancy, and a data analytics firm. As a member of the Forbes Business Council, she is recognized for her entrepreneurial achievements.

Her recruitment firm, RecruitGyan, aids tech startups in forming stellar teams, boasting a 92% fill rate and significantly reducing turnover. Neha's sleep consultancy, The Sleepy Cub, emphasizes the importance of sleep tailored to individual lifestyles and cultural nuances, a topic she deeply resonates with as a first-generation immigrant. While balancing her businesses and family life, she champions the belief that success begins with restful sleep.

Please reach out to her at neha.naik@recruitgyan.com and receive her gift—a free 15-minute networking session where you can ask her anything: https://nehaintro.youcanbook.me/.

DELANEY JENSEN-HAGER

$\mathcal{D}$ELANEY JENSEN is passionate about teaching others that disabilities don't have to stop you from living your life. Delaney was diagnosed with dyslexia, dyspraxia, dysgraphia, dyscalculia, generalized anxiety disorder, test anxiety, and obsessive-compulsive disorder at 17 years old.

Now, at 21, she is a CEO, a podcast co-host, and with the book in your hands, she is adding author to that list of achievements. Here is the kicker... she hasn't even graduated from college yet! She graduates in December with a degree in organizational sciences and a double minor in public relations and communications.

Connect with Delaney at https://www.vestatalks.com/dyslexic-with-delaney

DENISE BRUSCHI

$\mathcal{M}$ EET DENISE Bruschi, born and raised in Chicago, mother of four, and grandmother of seven. As a military wife of 18 years, she has shown amazing resilience, adaptability, and strength in the face of challenges.

Denise has a deep sense of justice and is an advocate of equality and empowerment. Her willingness to inspire and uplift others by sharing her experiences and wisdom helps women find their voices.

Contact her at:
Email: denisebruschi2@gmail.com
Website: denisebruschi.com

PATRICIA DIEUDONNE

*M*EET PATRICIA Dieudonne, a mom of two boys and a rambunctious dog, Rex, living in South Florida.

Born in the enchanting landscapes of Austria, Patricia relocated to the United States as a teenager. She received her bachelor's degree from the University of Central Florida but found a career in real estate, eventually becoming a real estate broker. After a bout with cancer, she went on a self-discovery journey and became a life coach with various certifications.

Patricia's mission is to help women find their passion and their purpose in creating a six-figure business without succumbing to overwhelm or burnout. Her goal is to ensure women entrepreneurs can still enjoy life with their families or loved ones.

Fun Facts about Patricia: She is fluent in five languages—English, German, Polish, Spanish, and Portuguese. When she is not coaching, you will most likely find her on the dance floor dancing the Salsa or Bachata.

Ready to embark on your own transformational journey? Connect with Patricia on Facebook and Instagram (@manifestwithpatricia) for a daily dose of inspiration. Dive into her world of wisdom and download free resources that will kickstart your remarkable transformation. For a deeper dive, visit her website: www.patriciadieudonne.com.

Your journey toward empowerment begins now. Let's manifest a brighter, bolder you—hand in hand!

KARLEEN WAGNER

KARLEEN IS a Colorado native and has been happily married for 28 years. She and her husband have two adult children and are currently enjoying life as empty nesters!

In 2011, a personal health crisis served as a wakeup call for her, prompting a significant lifestyle reevaluation. Her journey toward improved physical, mental and emotional wellbeing has given life to a new passion to help others move past merely surviving into a life where they thrive!

Her company, Choosing to Thrive, embodies the belief that we have a choice in how we show up in this world; we can choose to Thrive or just Survive. Visit her website for a free download of daily habits to help you create a life you love!

Contact:
Website: www.choosingtothrivellc.com
Email: karleenwagner@comcast.net
Facebook: https://www.facebook.com/ChoosingtoThriveLLC
Instagram: https://www.instagram.com/choosing_to_thrive_/

Made in the USA
Middletown, DE
06 November 2023